THE FLOW OF THE RIVER

Navigating your Personal and Professional Growth
Along The River Of Your Life
Using The Extraordinary Methodology of
Geo-Emotional Mapping

Ali Bagley & Marco Bertagni

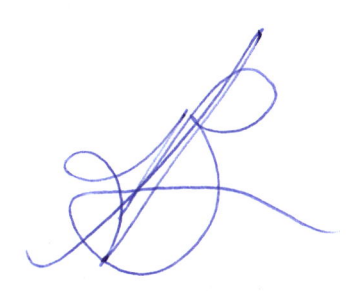

THE FLOW OF THE RIVER

Copyright © 2022 Ali Bagley and Marco Bertagni
All rights reserved.
ISBN: 9798758268537

DEDICATION

For Uberto, Anna, Eddy & Elizabeth

Thank you for bringing us into the world as children of 64
Thank you for giving us love, hope and the freedom to play

You came from the Earth
You are our Roots
You gave us Life
You shaped our Emotions
You encouraged our Philosophy
You gave us our Freedom

We are your legacy
We will honour you as we continue our journey
along the rivers of our lives

THE FLOW OF THE RIVER

CONTENTS

Chapter 1: welcome to the magical world of eliciting, mapping & managing emotions 3

Why we wrote this book 4
Sharing Knowledge – Our Ethos 4
Significance 6
Growth 7
    Growth as a Human Need 7
    Growth as an Emotional Reputation Strategy 7
Learning New Skills 9
    But how do you know what skills you still need to learn? 9
A Tool for Life and Your Business 10
How Emotional Geography Changes You 11
What You Will Get From This Book 14
International and Cross-cultural 14
For Individuals, Groups and Business 15
The EMME Community 15
How to Use This Book 16
MAPS 17

Chapter 2: Learning from the experts but who are they? 21

Marco's Story – A Journey of Growth & Friendship 21
The River of Life Project – Where it all began 25
The River of Life
Special Edition for You, right here, right now 31
Ali's Story – a Journey of Discovery and Freedom 46
The Lighthouse of Significance and Growth 50

Chapter 3: The Methodology 57

The History of Geo-Emotional Mapping (GEM) 57
Traditional Timeline Coaching v's GEM 58
Bringing GEM into the 21st Century 60
How Geo-Emotional Mapping Works 61
    The Methodology 61
    The Wheels 63
The Importance of Travel 65
Your Map 65
The Sharing 65
The Discoveries 66
Pack Your Luggage 66
Time to Draw Your Geo-Emotional River of Life Map 67
Analysis 67
    Time Distribution 67
    Physical Geography and Place Symbolism 67
    Sharing 67

CHAPTER 4: Seeing things from another perspective, unlocking the Secrets in your map 69

Self-Awareness 69
Third-Party Perception 69
Highlighting the Positives 69
Creating Your In-Depth Breakdown 70
Creating Your Action Plan for Success 70

CHAPTER 5: fearless - getting closer to your ambitions and dreams 72

From the River of Life to "Fearless" 73
THE TASTE OF GEO-EMOTIONS 78

CHAPTER 6: Problem solving - different applications for GEo-Emotional Mapping 82

Overview 82

For Life 83

For Business 83

For Career 84

For Relationships 84

For Health 85

For Legacy 85

For Recovery 86

For Family 86

For Travel 87

For Storytelling, Book Writing and Scripts 87

For Project Analysis 88

For Team Building 88

For Fun and Games 89

CHAPTER 7: Building a Community 91

EMME – The Community 91

What We Do 91

Why We Do It 91

How We Do It 92

Who We Are 92

Networking 93

Collaboration 93

CHAPTER 8: One to One or Group GEO-Emotional mapping as a tool to grow your business 95

As a Client 95

Benefits for your people and your business 96

Developing Bespoke Training for Your People 96

Growing Your Business Using Emotional Geography as a tool for your clients 96

Becoming a Geographer of Emotions 97

Becoming a Licensee 98

A USP for Your Business 98

Using Geo-emotional Geography to Build Your Community..... 98

CHAPTER 9: Having Fun 101

The Journeys 102

The Community... 103

GEM for Parties and Events 103

CHAPTER 10: Inspiring others - what is next for us and for you 105

2022 and Beyond 105

The Festival of Emotions 106

   How it Works 106

   What it seeks to Achieve.. 106

   The Layout 106

   The Opportunities For Individuals 107

   The Opportunities For Businesses 107

   The Opportunities For Schools and Colleges 107

   Book Your Place 107

Contact Us... 107

Sponsors and Supporters 109

THE FLOW OF THE RIVER

ACKNOWLEDGMENTS

A huge shout out to the Geographers of Emotions.
You shine a light in the world and make this dream a reality.
Thank you
All of our course, journey and game clients.
You came, you saw, you enjoyed and benefitted,
and we have loved having you here.
Bernie and Roberta, you put up with our crazy hours,
our madcap schemes and our need to dream.
Thank you for your support and love.

THE FLOW OF THE RIVER

CHAPTER 1: WELCOME TO THE MAGICAL WORLD OF ELICITING, MAPPING & MANAGING EMOTIONS

If you are looking for personal and professional growth and to gain more significance in your world, the secrets we reveal in this book are exactly what you need. This is both a fascinating read and an interactive workbook in which we show you how the methodology of Geo-Emotional Mapping works.

Developed by Marco Bertagni in 2016 and now at the heart of the International Coaching Platform he runs with Ali Bagley, Geo-Emotional Mapping (GEM), the methodology of Emotional Geography, has been used successfully in hundreds of courses, journeys and games, delivered into corporations, universities and schools and in one-to one coaching and training across the world.

You will learn all about this incredible methodology, how to use it for your own growth and significance as well as how to harness it for your employees and your business, either as a service or as a provider yourself.

Many people claim to have a unique approach, many more claim to be different. We know that what we are about to share with you is indeed unique, definitely different and for sure a book you will come back to again and again as you experience the ***Flow of the River*** of your life.

Why we wrote this book

Every time we introduce ourselves as Geographers of Emotions, at networking events, in training courses, actually at any kind of occasion where we are meeting new people, we always get the same set of responses, 'What's that then?', 'What do you do exactly?', 'So, what is Emotional Geography?'

Well as you can see from the contents page in this book, explaining what Emotional Geography is, and thus what it means to be a Geographer of Emotions, is not something we could easily condense into a simple response.

We tend to say that Emotional Geography is a methodology for personal and professional Growth and Significance that we deliver in multiple courses, journeys and games but goodness me that really is the very short version. And it always leads to more questions.

Now don't misunderstand us here, we LOVE talking about what we do and will hold you captive for hours on end waxing lyrical about the joys and benefits of the services we offer, the amazing results we have seen in our clients and the passion we have for emotional mapping.

Unfortunately, most people don't have that much time to spend in conversation with us and we also want to spread the word to as many people as possible. Hence the need for this book. You can learn all about what we do, why, and the amazing results we get, plus how to get them for yourself, in your own time and at your own pace.

Then you can contact us if you have any further questions!

Sharing Knowledge – Our Ethos

Emotional Geography UK LTD (the home of EMME) is an;

INTERNATIONAL NETWORK

of

SKILLED INDIVIDUALS

providing

PATHS of GROWTH

and

SIGNIFICANCE

through

EMOTIONAL GEOGRAPHY

Delivered, live and online, to Individuals, Companies, Schools, Universities and Organizations by Certified, Accredited and Master Geographers of Emotions, from 20 different Countries, sharing their expertise and emotions.

It began with the The River Of Life Project, a scientific art and an ethical system, built on respect for self, others and our planet. This project gave birth to EMME (Eliciting, Mapping & Managing Emotions) which is now a part of as EMOTIONAL GEOGRAPHY UK LTD.

OUR OBJECTIVES are to empower and enrich lives by providing Personal and Professional Growth and Significance services using the methodology of Geo-Emotional Mapping in our:

CONSULTING

COACHING

COUNSELLING

JOURNEYS

&

RIVER GAMES

OUR CHARTER

We, as citizens of the World and friends of EMME come together to share our knowledge, our skills, our compassion and our experience. In doing so, we respect the philosophy of **E**liciting, **M**apping and **M**anaging **E**motions, ensuring that our clients become better informed, better skilled and satisfied with the experiences they have had with us. We seek to help others to grow and enrich their lives through the harnessing of their emotional energy in order to facilitate their desired change.

Significance

The dictionary describes Significance as, *'the quality of being worthy of attention; importance.'*

As human beings we all want to be worthy of attention, we all want to be important, do we not?

So, what makes us attention worthy, what makes us important? The list is probably endless but here are a few examples for you to think about:

- Having an impressive job title
- Doing something above and beyond the usual
- Being a support to someone else
- Helping others to achieve a life change
- Being a decision maker
- Being uniquely you
- Being loveable
- Being depended upon
- Being well known in our field
- Being talented
- Making others feel good
- Being the best at something
- Having a flash car
- Standing out in a crowd
- Getting a promotion
- Having something no-one else has

We are sure you can think of many more than this but just based on this list, which would you say are the most important?

There are no rights or wrong here, it is just opinion. What is clear is that to achieve many of the things on this list we need certain skills, certain attributes and attitudes and a good dollop of knowledge.

We understand that significance is a key driver for the majority of our clients. You want to be well known, stand out from the crowd, be the best, be known for your success. That might be in your personal life, in your relationships and social activities, or it might be in your professional life, in your career or business.

All of our services are designed with growing your significance in mind. Providing you with those skills that you need, working on your attributes and attitudes and giving you our years of experience in the form of knowledge, processes and tools that you can use to grow your success.

Growth

Growth as a Human Need

Are you always pushing boundaries – your own and those set for you by other people? Are you independent and driven? Do you sometimes find it hard to connect with others, moving on quickly from relationships? If so, Growth could be the human need that motivates you most.

If **Growth** is your top human need, you are always striving to be better and learn more. You are very good at your job but tend to move on as soon as you believe you've reached your full potential. Although your constant striving for improvement means you'll never be bored, you can be a bit of a perfectionist, giving you high levels of stress in your life and work.

Is **Growth** your key motivator?

Growth as an Emotional Reputation Strategy

While there are six Emotional Reputation Strategies, (as developed by Chantal Cornelius of Apple Tree Marketing Services and detailed further in Chapter 8) most businesses will have just one that will really help them to attract their ideal clients.

When **Growth** is your Emotional Reputation Strategy, clients will work with you because they know that you can help either them or their business to grow. Many coaches work with clients who are looking for personal growth – they need help to move beyond the obstacles that are in their path, or they need support on their journey. They might be stuck and unable to see their own potential, so will work with a coach who can help them to develop their own skills and confidence.

Other coaches, as well as many consultants and mentors, help clients with the growth of their business. As a Marketing Consultant, Chantal is often approached by potential clients who are struggling to grow their businesses. Sales Consultants can help their clients to grow too, by showing them how to convert more of their prospects into clients. Training companies can also help their clients to grow – both personally and in a business context.

Growth is a key driver for us here at Emotional Geography UK Ltd, for ourselves as well as our clients.

Here is what Chantal had to say about us:

> "My favourite example of a business using **Growth** as their Emotional Reputation Strategy is a company I've recently started working with, called Emotional Geography UK Ltd. Previously going by another name, (EMME) this company had a catalogue of over 150 training courses
>
> that clients could choose from. These covered a very diverse range of topics, from The Non-Sexist City (Gender Studies) and Couples Therapy based on traditional Psychology, to Connecting People (Theatre as an emotional bridge) to my personal favourite – Searching for Beauty (Clown Therapy and Self-Irony)! Can you see a link between any of those courses?
>
> The link is actually the methodology used in all of the courses – a brilliantly clever technique called Emotional Mapping. The company thought that was how they should promote their courses. The problem with offering 150 courses to your clients, with no visible link or theme, is that you just overwhelm them. Too much choice often leaves clients making no buying choice at all.
>
> When I spent some time working with Emotional Geography, we realised that their Emotional Reputation Strategy is actually **Growth**. Their most popular courses are ones that help their clients to grow. The company has now reduced

the list of courses, focusing purely on the ones that make the lives of their clients better. The course descriptions will be rewritten to show prospects how each course can help them or their business to grow. Its early days, but when Emotional Geography shared this new strategy with their service leads and moderators, there was unanimous buy in and support."

Learning New Skills

As human beings we are predisposed to search for knowledge, to develop new skills, to gain understanding and to hear new stories. It is in our nature to be inquisitive and to grow.

Just look at our history. Inventors, explorers, truth seekers, writers, philosophers and poets. All human beings searching beyond the known horizons in an attempt to find a better place, a better future, a better way.

In our own way, we are all inventors, explorers and travellers. We love to have new experiences, see new things, learn new things and through all of that enrich our lives and grow as individuals.

We are storytellers. We communicate in stories. Knowledge gives us material for our stories, makes us interesting and keeps us entertained.

But how do you know what skills you still need to learn?

Sometimes we take a bit of a hap hazard approach to deciding which new skills we want to learn. Maybe you get the chance of a free training course at work, so you take it, more out of curiosity than need. Perhaps you have started a new business and so jump onto every webinar or free 'masterclass' in the hope that you will learn enough to make your business a success.

In truth this approach is often costly and time consuming for very little growth in your skill set.

We all know we need and want to learn new skills do we not? So surely, it's a great idea to find a way to understand exactly what you need to learn and why, in order to achieve specific goals. In fact, even to define what those goals are first?

Well, you are in luck because the first journey everybody takes with Emotional Geography is to develop their River of Life Map. A map that will show you how far you have come, define where you want to go, highlight the lessons you have learned that serve you well and identify the gaps in your skill set that you need to fill to move forward.

Sounds ambitious? Maybe, but it works.

> *"Your approach is really inspiring. Looking back to my story from the real beginning and watching at all the troubles and challenges I was passing through, it really boosts my self-confidence and make me more sure about the next goals for my family, my business and my career."* Michele Preti, Entrepreneur

A Tool for Life and Your Business

"Discovery is the journey; insight is the destination."
Gary Hamel

Your River of Life Map, (indeed once you start you can't stop so you will also develop maps for your business, your relationships, your career, and many other variations for every challenge you need insight to solve) is more than just a map, it is insight, self-awareness and clarity.

More than anything your River of Life Map is, **INSIGHT**.

What do we mean by that? Insight, the ability to see 'inside'. The dictionary definition is, '*the capacity to gain an accurate and deep understanding of someone or something*'.

When we talk about emotional mapping the key words we would point out here are 'accurate' and 'deep'.

Here are a few thoughts on insight . . .

"Insight must precede application."

Max Planck

There is nothing so terrible as activity without insight.

Thomas Carlyle

"Insight without action is worthless."

Marie Forleo

"Self-examination is the key to insight, which is the key to wisdom."

M. Scott Peck

That last one nails it . . . self-examination is the key to insight.

Would you agree that it is often difficult to see situations and challenges from a logical / objective / detached point of view when you are slap bang in the middle of said situation or event? Certainly, it's difficult to see things accurately and deeply is it not?

So, this tool for your life and your business, Geo-Emotional Mapping, it is an insightful tool for self-examination that gives you accurate and deep understanding of a particular situation, challenge or relationship.

It does this by enabling you to see things from a third party, objective and detached point of view. With clarity.

With that understanding you can then begin to solve the problem, overcome the challenge, grow your skills, become stronger and move forward to a more successful and significant future.

How Emotional Geography Changes You

We tell you our stories of how Emotional Geography has completely changed our lives for the better in the next chapter.

The changes that this methodology makes in people is very personal, but we will attempt to condense that down into a succinct overview for you.

In our experience, working with hundreds of people using geo-emotional mapping in our courses, games and journeys these are the key changes we see:

Increased confidence – the knowledge that 'yes, I can do this'.

Better clarity – particularly for understanding what actually has happened and what needs to happen next.

Growing belief – realising that we are more than we might have thought before.

Acceptance – of situations that were bringing us down before.

The ability to plan – through understanding what we really want and need we can set targeted goals and a clear path towards them.

New Businesses conceived – ideas generated from a new sense of awareness.

Growth – as a human being, leader, communicator and as part of a team.

Significance – in business, in life, in relationships, and in self-worth.

Here is a selection of testimonials from attendees on our courses, journeys and games, all of whom have found Geo-emotional Mapping life-changing in both their personal and professional lives:

Inspiring
Aneesa Chaudhry

Hi Marco
Thank you for today's session. It was really beautifully presented and insightful. It made me smile on the inside and I found the method of connecting with emotion through drawing, inspiring.

Collaborating
Ivy Barreto

Collaborating with Ali has been quite exhilarating, her entrepreneurial approach, work ethics and professionalizing with an empathetic touch, has been quite an exquisite experience. Looking forward to many more ventures together in embracing the masses in dreaming BIG.

Inspiring
Michele Preti

Your approach is really inspiring. Looking back to my story from the beginning, and seeing the troubles and challenges I was passing through, it really boosted my self confidence and make me more sure about the next goals for my family, my business and my career.

Collaborating
Marco Barozzi

I'd like to tell you that I much enjoyed your course, starting from mapping my emotions to retrace my professional career and make plans for the future. So, thank you again for delivering such an interesting course. It was fun, insight and learning, all at the same time.

Heart & Soul
Marie-Anna Reck

I feel that this project Emme has touched me where it is needed direct to my heart and soul I resonate with your principles and ideas and would love to grow with it and establish venues and paths ahead

Great Session
Marcia Hylton

Great session tonight, loved it and learned so much, thank you.

Great Session
Bernd Gibson

The session yesterday afternoon was very powerful and inspiring. I particularly liked they way you two involved the audience in a passive, non-aggressive way without putting anybody on the spot.
I'd love to see how this journey continues

Immense & Intense
Aisha Chaudhry

I did this journey. It was an immense and intense experience that opened my eyes to connecting a place I wanted to explore with creating an imaginary journey that made me delve deep into my own journey in life. What's not to love about that!

> **Huge Fun**
> Ailsa Tulloch
>
> What huge fun. I think we should bring storytelling into all our presentations. The whole experience was a flight of imagination and humour. Perhaps, we should create a crazy storytelling group? Love you all. Goodnight and watch out for dragons.

> **Creative Approach**
> Susan Lane
>
> This creative approach is focused on freeing and empowering your inner writer to share your message. The step by step program helps organize your thoughts and gets you writing from day 1. Lots of great advice and guidance to take the angst out of getting started

What You Will Get From This Book

You are going to get the secrets of Geo-Emotional Geography, how it works, how to use it for yourself and how to use it to grow your business.

You are going to get information on the various courses journeys and games we have developed for your growth and significance and how you can access them, or even develop them yourself!

You are going to be able to create your own maps, analyse them and use the insights you gain to become more successful and fulfilled.

You will be invited to join us as we move forward on our journey with the Festival of Emotions and the EMME community.

International and Cross-cultural

Everything about emotional geography is truly international and cross cultural. Let's begin with the Geographers of Emotions, over 80 of us from all over the world, from different cultures, speaking different languages and working in really diverse industries and businesses.

We work together harmoniously with no boundaries for one good reason.

Emotions are unilateral, we all have them, we all feel them, and emotional geography allows us to process them in our own individual way for our own individual reasons.

There is no competition, no divides. We are a truly international group made up of citizens of the world.

One of the great things to come from this is the knowledge and understanding we have gained from that cross-cultural working. This has led to the development of a number of services to help you to create a better understanding of diversity, managing inter-cultural teams and products, developing better international trade relations and collaboration to name but a few.

For Individuals, Groups and Business

What we do in helping you to grow and become more significant through emotional geography works on a one-to-one basis and for groups of individuals coming together with similar interests, challenges or goals.

It also has many applications for business, for leadership and management, communication, team work and project management.

In fact, if there is emotion involved then whether it's for individuals, groups, teams or corporations then it works as a methodology for growth and significance.

The EMME Community

As part of this chapter, we must introduce you to the community of Eliciting, Mapping and Managing Emotions, aka EMME.

EMME is an international and experiential network made up of Geographers of Emotions, who are inviting People and Organizations to join a multifaceted and unique journey.

We come from many countries of the world, as you can see from this map:

COUNTRIES OF ORIGIN OF EMME'S GEOGRAPHERS OF EMOTIONS

Our dream, purpose, will and ambition are to help you rediscover your own vocation, to elicit, map out, live, share and recognise emotions, and to build soft and hard skills, through the provision of our courses, journeys and games.

You can access all of our services and support through The Festival of Emotions: www.emotional-geography.com where you will also find our extended community which includes:

The EMME – Geographers of Emotions Facebook group - https://www.facebook.com/groups/213734233615058

Our weekly networking call - open to anyone with an interest in growth and significance

And

Our LinkedIn page – EMME Courses, Consultancy and Counselling - https://www.linkedin.com/company/emme-courses-consultancy-and-counseling

We are over 80 Geographers of Emotions, with almost 500 FB group members and followers on LinkedIn.

Come on in and be a part of it.

How to Use This Book

What do you want?

If it's just our story, then read Chapter 2 and decide what to do after that

If it's to learn about and use Emotional Geography for your personal and professional growth and significance, then read on after Chapter 2 right up to the end of Chapter 6.

If it all the above plus wanting to know more about our community, how to use emotional geography as a part of your business strategy, how to use it for fun and what happens next, well, just keep reading.

This book is a journey, how far you want to travel with us is totally up to you, as is everything we do in Emotional Geography.

MAPS

Just to give you a flavour of what a Geo-emotional Map looks like, here are the first ones Marco and I did.

Plus, if you go onto YouTube here you can see loads of them in full technicolour, with music! https://youtu.be/orY9NmTjgik

THE FLOW OF THE RIVER

Marco's Map

THE FLOW OF THE RIVER

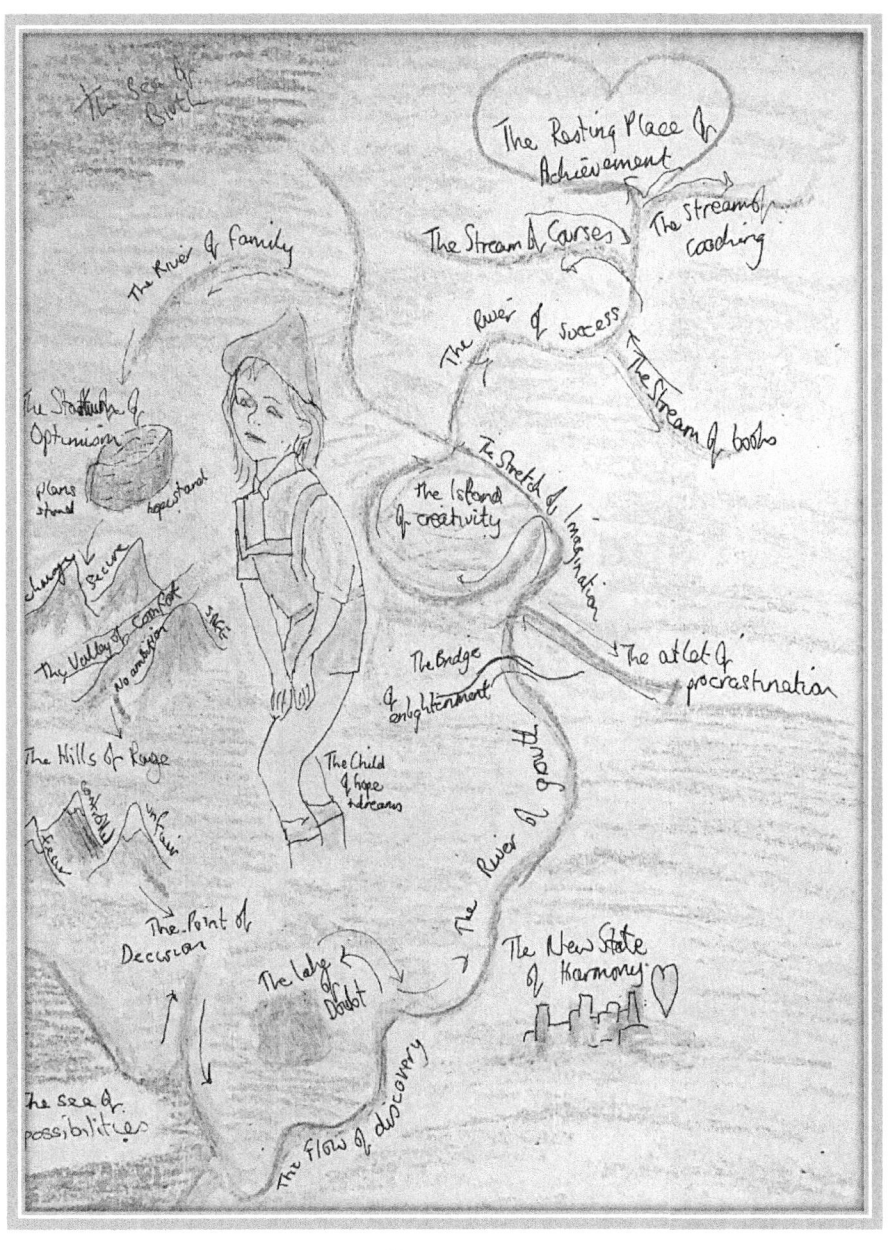

Ali's Map

THE FLOW OF THE RIVER

CHAPTER 2: LEARNING FROM THE EXPERTS BUT WHO ARE THEY?

Marco's Story – A Journey of Growth & Friendship

The secrets of transforming rainy days into sunny days. Or ... how to understand the rain.

On a rainy day in November 2008, a tall man, with a nice smile, according to what his mother Anna used to say, was working as a Managing Director of an Industrial Association, when he was suddenly laid off.

They told him not to take it personally because the decision had been made due to the economic and financial crisis of 2008. He was so choked at hearing this, that he could barely register the pathetic explanations of a decision, that to him sounded deeply unjust.

After the initial paralysis, followed by anger, sadness, disgust and fear, the tall man, who had lost his smile for a while and whose name is Marco by the way, gradually made room for different kinds of thoughts, not far from joy.

"What if this unexpected and unfair event was my sliding door towards new horizons?"

It was January 2009 when he decided to go travelling to Greece, inspired by 'Ulysses Gaze' by Angelopulos. He needed to go somewhere else, alone, to gain a different viewpoint on his professional life, and search for a new beginning.

Through a snowy Epirus, Marco reached the valley of Meteora and... yes!, on the top of a Meteora, while watching the sun rising, he understood that things are not just black or white, they change their meaning according to the meaning we give them. Marco got his smile back.

On February 13th, 2009, once back in Italy, he founded Bertagni Consulting srl, a company dealing with International Trade and Lobbying.

In the first 6 years of activity, thanks to the help of many friends from different Countries, the Bertagni Consulting 'Team' thrived. They developed international markets, through travelling and strengthening relations with the EU Commission and domestic Administrations, delivering an effective and ethical lobbying policy for the industrial sectors they represented.

On October 16th 2015, Marco, who had also by then graduated in Geographical Sciences with a thesis on Emotional Cartography, finished drawing his geo-emotional map.

Inspired by the map, charting his journey along his river, Marco wrote a book called THE RIVER OF LIFE: another turning point of his life.

His initial realisation, through maps, lyrics and pictures – was that his journey into the Geography of Emotions had given him relief on so many levels and brought him a great and harmonious feeling of joy.

Then, inspired by the values that he integrated in the story – respect, perspectives, vocation, dreaming, listening, knowledge, geographical thinking – he began to create River-connected activities: seminars, workshops, artistic events, journeys and performances.

Little by little emotional geography became part of daily activities of Bertagni Consulting, and gave birth to what has become, and will continue to be more and more in the future, the core business of the company: Significance and Growth through Emotional Geography.

When, in November 2019, Marco founded EMME, (Eliciting, Mapping & Managing Emotions) Ulysses again came to mind.

In Chapter XXVI of Inferno, Dante writes about Ulysses and tells us about when the hero decided to leave Itaca to go searching for knowledge with his companion:

Ulysses:

> *"I and my company were old and slow*
> *When at the narrow passage we arrived*
> *Where Hercules his landmarks set as signals,*
> *That man no farther onward should adventure.*
> *On the right hand behind me left I Seville,*
> *And on the other already had left Ceuta.*
> *'O brothers, who amid a hundred thousand*
> *Perils', I said, 'have come unto the West,*
> *To this inconsiderable vigil*
> *Which is remaining of your senses still*
> *Be ye unwilling to deny the knowledge,*
> *Following the sun, of the unpeopled world.*
> *Consider ye the seed from which ye sprang;*
> **Ye were not made to live like unto brutes,**
> **But for pursuit of virtue and of knowledge'.**

EMME, was then in Marco's eyes, a metaphorical boat sailing

towards a deeper Knowledge, and he felt from the very beginning that he was not alone on that boat but surrounded by many friends.

On December 30th, 2020 Bertagni Consulting officially launched EMME: with 64 Geographers of Emotions, coming from 14 different Countries and bringing multiple skills, insights, experience and knowledge.

What is important about those 64 (now 80+ and increasing) is this: they are human beings, seeking to share their skills and experiences in order to build and develop a bespoke, but at the same time common knowledge to help our clients to reach their personal and professional goals by following their vocation and by growing into who they are meant to be.

> *What is curious about these 64 is this: Marco, crazy for unusual statistics, decided to select and weigh the Latitude and Longitude values of the Capital Cities of the Countries where the original 64 came from and the average values were 38°N - 1°E . . . which is in the Mediterranean Sea, in between Ceuta and Sevilla facing the Strait of Gibraltar: right in the very same place where Dante 700 hundreds years ago placed Ulysses and his companions in the Divina Commedia! Just a coincidence? Marco does not think so.*

Not long ago, in January 2021, on one of the few cold mornings of Anzio during the whole year, Marco as usual, was walking on the Tirrena beach, starting his day by watching the sunrise.

The Circeo Promontory was surprisingly clear at the horizon.

How not to think, once more to Ulysses and his journeys.

In that very moment a boat of fishermen stopped between Marco, the Circeo and the rising sun.

Marco was moved.

He though: "Yes, like Ulysses, I made mistakes in my life, some choices were wrong, but I never lost my passion for life, I am still and more and more in love with life. And I am not alone in this journey of Growth and Friendship".

In the afternoon of the same day, the weather turned grey and, unexpectedly, started to rain.

Marco went out and stood in the rain. He didn't get wet.

He simply felt and enjoyed each single drop of rain.

The River of Life Project – Where it all began

Marco, the boy with the suitcase

For many years, Marco's aunt Diana had told him about a lost picture that portrayed him as a three-year-old, smiling, with a suitcase in his hand.

"There's your essence in that picture", she told him.

In 2013, a few days after his aunt's death, while rummaging through a trunk amongst hundreds of pictures, Marco came across that image: short pants, straps, a suitcase bigger than him.

Diana was right. That picture, which represented a departure, a journey, a moment of happiness, was…Marco, the child with the suitcase.

Marco now likes to believe that his thirst for knowledge of the world was born at that moment, when his father Umberto took that picture in 1967.

September 13th, 2015, was another important day for Marco. It would have been his mother Anna's eighty-sixth birthday. He was in Anzio, sat at his desk, looking at the sea waiting for the sun to dawn among the palm trees. He wondered: 'Why did I travel that much? Why do I still want to travel? What does it mean "knowledge of the World"? Does "to know" mean "to connect knowledges"? "To go beyond what we see"? And what is life? What do I want it to be? Is there something before and after?'

The thoughts became so intense that he felt the need to get them out, projected from his mind and onto paper. The question was how? How can a life, made up of unlimited and always moving elements, be represented? How can inner landscapes be represented?

So, inattentively and half dreaming, he began to draw swift blue lines on a blank sheet of paper, not sure what he was drawing. As he drew, he reflected, 'what if life is a journey through the geography of emotions, looking for the soul of the World and one's own? The journey flows, like water in a river, and so does life. Journey, emotions, river, water, movement, life…'

For Marco this was a 'Eureka!' moment. That first blue line took the shape of a river to which, in the following days, he added a number of fictional geographical names that – as in the Carte du Pays de Tendre by Madeleine de Scudéry – symbolised his feelings and shaped his emotions in a topographical way.

By the 16th of October 2015, he had finished drawing this curious map, and divided it into six Regions – Earth, Roots, Emotions,

Life, Philosophy and Freedom, studded with imaginary toponyms.

He felt that he had created a kind of mould, a paradigmatic structure, a geographical archetype that was – at least in his eyes – an implicit invitation to the journey, to an existential journey through places where we could project and anchor our own past, dreams and fears and from which to receive strong feelings and messages to decode.

This was the beginning of Marco's journey through the geography of the Valley of Existence.

This "open" and unreal journey, since he constantly swung between dimensions – a physical one, related to the flow of time, where he used his memory in order to connect to places – and an inner dimension, a dreamlike, non-spatial and timeless one, based on imagination and evocation in order to redirect and integrate his emotions, to explore unknown lands and to take a leap of faith into his inner self.

A "philosophical" journey, because he thought long on the meaning of life, on the importance of the exchange and the dialogue, on the need to deploy the knowledge and on the appearances of reality.

As he took this metaphysical journey along the river of his life, Marco contemplated his place in the world.

Walking through the **Earth** he imagined the World before Man and he felt like "a small seed of man", infinitely small faced with the magnificence of Mother Earth. He thought about how many men believe they can dominate the Universe rather than restrict themselves to recognising its greatness and harmony.

In **Roots,** he saw the faces of his ancestors, listened to their stories and understood the continuation of life through the generations.

In **Emotions,** he was up, then down, getting breathless in the Lake of the Stolen Dreams, where he met Lorenzo Guarnieri, a boy whose life has been taken when he was just 17 years old. There he decided that one of the objectives of his journey – in addition to knowing the world and himself – was to understand if there was a way to close Lorenzo's loop, interrupted one night in

June 2010. He thought about loss and about finding a way to be reborn. He was angry about the injustice and cruelty of people who take other people's freedom because they don't respect Man and Life.

In **Life**, he travelled the Waters of experience to understand the world, not just to look at it. He faced responsibilities and choices, observed the good and the bad. He felt himself to be, as was everyone else, in the big Island of Shadows and Lights.

In **Philosophy**, he combined reason and passion because he understood that awareness comes from the combination of these two ingredients. He imagined being on the Philosophy Peak while illustrating The River of Life.

From there, memory made way again for imagination, he wanted a better world, where harmony reigned, where man was integrated with Mother Earth; he dreamed of breathing the spirit of the places.

In **Freedom**, as if by magic, he found closure and, from the invisible loops that wrap around the Universe, he felt blessed with warming energy.

As a result of his journey, mapping his thoughts, experiences and revelations, Marco found a deep and profound understanding of who he is and what guides him in his life. As if he had opened that suitcase and put all of its contents in order.

He had looked beyond the clouds and, in front of the Timeless Sunrise Promontory, he felt a new beginning.

In this storytelling of his life, he had laid his feelings bare, shaping his inner landscapes by anchoring them to real and imaginary places, listening to what each place had to say. He felt like he was walking, lightly, on the imaginary ridge that links the points where the two flows of the geography of emotions meet: the one which is projected outside from inside, and the one that arises from real places and impacts on our thoughts.

He "fulfilled his soul", dreaming of becoming a geographer of emotions and knowing a little more about the soul of the World and about his own soul.

Since that initial journey in 2015 Marco has continued to develop the principles of geo-emotional mapping as a tool for everyone looking towards personal and professional development.

During the initial drafting of the narrative of this project, he once awoke, startled, at 5 am because he physically needed to immediately add a given place in the River of Life tale, particular pictures that he had taken on his travels through Cambodia, Greenland, Patagonia, Indonesia and other places.

It was a gentle, stimulating and cathartic process of surfacing and harmonisation of pictures, images, words, but, above all, of life moments, emotional splinters, sensations felt at the most diverse latitudes in his lifetime.

This in turn became the book, The River of Life, published in 2016. A philosophical book, where the words and pictures leave the reader in contemplation of more than the story they tell for Marco.

The River of Life means this for Marco.

"What I most desire is that The River of Life leads you to believe that this River is mine but also yours. Just as your River is also mine."

Three things for every River of Life traveller to consider:

1. We are not alone in this World. If, on the one hand, this irrefutable fact consoles us, on the other hand it must make us realize that our freedom ends where another person's freedom begins. If we don't love and respect those living on Earth with us, our lives only serve to deprive those who do live loving and

respectful lives of their oxygen.
2. While travelling through the Valley, never lose sight of the source of the River; the source gives meaning, direction and colour to our existence. It is from the source, wherever that may be, that we have to start in order to direct our life towards our dreams.
3. Stop whenever possible and look at the river. See all the little things that travel with us, everything that is going on in the waters, and listen to the flow as it passes by.

The River of Life project was born and over the last six years has grown into EMME – Eliciting, Mapping & Managing Emotions.

The River of Life
Special Edition for You, right here, right now

THE RIVER OF LIFE

A journey through the geography of emotions.

Marco Bertagni

EARTH
The genesis of the World

I'm Marco.

I always have been.
I think I will always be.

A small seed of man carried by the wind,
vaulting on a land virgin of any humanity.
I perceive primordial lights.

THE FLOW OF THE RIVER

Forceful rivers gush out from ageless chasms,
a motionless extension of deserts offers mind-blowing forms.
A seed of me, alone in that immensity,
plunged in extravagant colours and rocked by a gentle breeze.

Suddenly the serenity of place is shattered:

Mors tua vita mea, the evidence of life surrenders to death.
A shudder of terror plunges me into the night of time.

Eternal dawn comes to free me.
I am sheltered in a cave.
Hands are painted on the walls.
I am a little seed at the edge of humanity.

ROOTS

Who we are?

I perceive the ancestral stream...

A man, a woman, farmers' faces, an inner light,
the smile of little Anna.
A man, a woman, an uncertain future, a loaded gun,
the cry of little Uberto.

THE FLOW OF THE RIVER

Two streams flow into one , embrace each other:
Anna and Uberto.
A groan, I'm here,
Marco.

The family, a protective fence, the territory of the first steps in life.
Papà, Mamma, never-ending help, a message of love:
"Marcolino, you will need to make your own Way,
take your suitcase and travel the world."

A journey, a deep emotion.

EMOTIONS

The geography of soul

I breath, I feel, I notice...
I unravel the thread of my existence and experience emotions that either raise me, or devastate me.

Emotions are everywhere.

Visible or hidden,
they live in all glances and give substance to our being.

THE FLOW OF THE RIVER

For some, the thread breaks, dreams are lost forever,
despite the caress of the sun.

For others, Earth moves away and,
deprived of anchorage by evil souls,
they are doomed to drift on waters now muddied by pain.

Like that little child,
dispossessed of his Ball, to whom,
without knowing why,
they have stolen the dreams and submerged illusions.
I want to bring the boats back to port.
I want to give the Ball back to the child.

LIFE
The waters of Experience

I feel a like a seed, Marco and yet a seed,
the wheel spins...

Like the child who believes in Santa Claus,

I remain astonished at my discoveries.

Like young people, excessive and thoughtless,

I pursue my dreams and,

unbeknownst to me,

I am looking for a flowering bougainvillea.

THE FLOW OF THE RIVER

A dam on the horizon, the reality recaptures me,
I have to stand up and face the responsibilities.

The stream increases.

Life intensifies.

Sirens multiply.

I learn to listen,
I swim in the experience of those who suggest I draw my path in the light of Respect.
I feel myself progressing in the construction of my free will and,
in spite of the slippery slope,
I shall keep myself upright;
before each fork I show signs of discernment.
I walk, I grow,

I belong to this humanity searching for bread between Eros and Thanatos.

I admire those who smile at life and who give smiles,
who find the time to give it to others,

those not swallowed by the pain.

I blame those who are not willing to listen and,
for distraction, arrogance or malice,
remove the light for others.
This way catapulted into the karstic waters of injustice,
they condemn themselves to remain in the darkness of existence.

They will need to awaken their consciences to regain the crystal clear and salvational waters leading to respect.

PHILOSOPHY
Looking for Happiness

I cross a bridge on which I reflect on my life,
but the tumult of the waters is too close and disturbs my thoughts.

THE FLOW OF THE RIVER

I go on looking for a peak propitious to a broader understanding of my existence.
Once reason makes room for heart,
I get kidnapped by far away rhythms.
I dance.

On the trail of my emotional geographies.

Then silence and vision.
I understand that losing means growing.
I wish faceless people to cope with a mirror, nothing else.
I would stop and listen.
The river, myself and souls.
And then leaving, changed.
I do not want to stop at appearances.
Life does not give gifts to those who turn their backs to her.

North South East West.
It is here where I am now.
I would like to endlessly orient myself.
Becoming who I was, I am and will be.
A child with the suitcase, but also a man who throws different glances at the world to quench his thirst for knowledge.
Or to increase it.

I am with humanity, hunting harmony.
I Imagine the man released from his prejudices.
I imagine his peaceful city, where he could rest.
I imagine him invaded by the spirit of places.
The imagery meets the reality, the horizon widens.
I see the sea in the distance.

FREEDOM

Lorenzo
I reach the sea, at dusk.
I perceive that I have to keep tracking my journey,
the lighthouse will be my inner light and dawn my eternal companion.
Far away from a bright light that dazzles everything,
I see now those little events that are the spice of life;
a window opens onto a flowering bougainvillea.
I admire its harmony and strength,
in silence and longing for my mother ...
Saudade.
Old son, I sculpted my soul out of the primordial magma;
the mind wrapped in the womb, I feed instinct with dreams.
My thoughts are gently tossed by waves and palm trees,
when I hear shrill and excited voices.

A child is playing.
His supple body traces acrobatic forms that open new perspectives.
He sees the sky in doing so.

The ball whirls from one World to another until it makes a hole in the clouds and reaches the child whose Life was stolen.
This ball is what you would have become, Lorenzo.
Take it and play with us number 10!
We need you.

The suitcase
I open my suitcase. For the first time. A globe.
Images of a departure and crystal-clear waters between huge rocks.
26 magical letters that, like crazy petals, float, held aloft by the breadth of knowledge, allowing the blossoming of the endless rose of humanity.
A blue thread that draws existential arabesques.
Pieces of a mosaic that, as if by magic, join to form a map.
The River of Mother, the Lake of Stolen Dreams, the Bridge of Awareness, the Sea of Freedom, the Promontory of Eternal Dawn and more...
Strange toponymes give birth within me to a feeling of deja vu.
Names evoking ancestral lands and lands of emotions.
Places that have been trampled, touched, smelled, felt.
Boara Polesine, the Garfagnana, the Serchio, Anzio, Alfama.
The whole World seen from a window of the Soul.
I turn round and round this strange map and find that all forms seem to contain another,
My vision of things evolves endlessly.

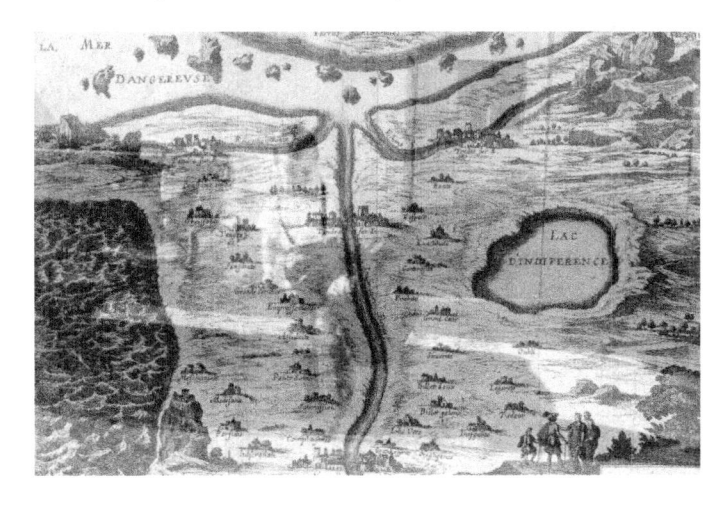

I rejoice because I am still the child inexorably attracted by the turning World.
The child who has not lost the will to wonder.
In the suitcase he has carefully preserved its Polar Stars,
his thirst for the World,
his Values,
his Dreams,
his Emotions.
The child who believed he carried his suitcase was instead guided by it.
To search for the soul of places.
And for his own.

Beyond the Clouds

Grapes, separated from the shoots by the hands of my ancestors become over time must, wine, spirit.
Life, with the passing of years, becomes a thousand lives.
The man, a thousand men.
I put the nectars of my age,
some sweet, others bitter,
in an alembic.
Out of this alchemical marriage an essence is generated
Transparent.
Very aromatic.
Music without false notes.
I am flooded by energy.
I drink of it.
I would like to have more,
but excess turns intelligence into presumption,
beauty into ugliness,
life into death.
The many Marcos are living together now and travelling along the new path of awareness, the deepest,
in this autumnal forest of existence.
I wish nothing more than to share this and continue to grow.
Making new discoveries.
Living mythically chasing my Daimon.
A shiver of cold wind will one day kidnap the bottle from my

hands.
Its flight, likewise a shot in the night, will last an interminable and obscure second.
Whale will take it, she will go under the blue mountain and leave it in the depths.
Perhaps the bottle will resurface.
Someone might find it.
There is the essence of my life inside it, my reason for being, forever.
Or up to there.
In the Sea of Freedom meanwhile, the sun of a new genesis arose.

THE END (THE BEGINNING)

To Lorenzo, Monica, Anna, Uberto and all those who are in a timeless place, simply writing another chapter of their River of Life, of our River of Life.

They are my family, our family.

All photographs and images in this book are copyright of Marco Bertagni and Emotional Geography UK ltd. And may not be reproduced without permission

Ali's Story – a Journey of Discovery and Freedom

When Ali looks back on her life, as she has often since discovering Emotional Geography, she realises that right now, in any given moment, she is a survivor of all that went before.

Her river has been a very winding one with many highs and many lows. From a childhood full of love and possibilities, into the angst of her overweight teenage years. From the hope of a marriage and children in her early twenties that ended in the despair of betrayal and a life of fear.

She built a new life, tried many careers, found a new love and moved on. Up and down, round and around.

In her fifties, happy in her personal life, in her career she found herself caught in a

The little girl with the big dreams

corporate hell hole where her years of experience and knowledge were valued far less than youth and the ability to be 'moulded'. She loved the work, but the environment was toxic and her mental, and thus her physical health, began to decline rapidly.

While she was away from work on sick leave Covid arrived and everything changed for everybody.

It gave her (very much younger) boss the chance to get rid of her through redundancy. That gave Ali the chance to escape and build the business she had always dreamed of. Win-Win.

Ali had always loved writing and the creative experience of storytelling, and she knew she was good at it. She also had years of business experience and oodles of corporate coaching and mentoring under her belt. Now how to bring all that together in a business?

Starting out full of dreams and excitement, newly certified after weeks of training to coach, and wanting to help as many people as she could Ali posted all over social media about her new venture, told family and friends, joined multiple networking groups and nothing . . . maybe a couple of calls . . . a few enquiries . . . but as with most new coaches, not a lot happened.

There she was, Ali Bagley Coaching, website built, a million ideas. She had no idea how much time and work it would take to build relationships, create a really solid service and begin making a living. Thank goodness for the redundancy pay-out. She had 12 months to make things happen.

Ali is now an established, respected, and busy coach earning a good living from her practice, her courses and her books. It has taken time, resilience, hard work and determination to get there. She couldn't have done it as a part time venture. She went all in. We are talking 12-hour days, weekend working, and doing stuff that needed to be done to enable her to do the stuff she loves.

Besides the long hours and hard work? This is what she did:

Step 1. Ali never, ever lost faith in herself and her ability to make her business a success.

She believes that the moment you lose faith, lose your confidence, people can tell. When you communicate with potential clients, they might be able to sense your desperation. People are attracted to confident successful people, it's a fact. You have to show the world that you are that person, all the time.

Step 2. She made sure that she had the financial means to survive without income for a year

Seriously, if you are the main breadwinner and you don't have the savings / money in the bank to back up the growth of your business then your options are limited to loans (not advisable unless you have step one absolutely cracked) and charity from friends and family. She had her redundancy money, it was enough, just to pay the bills for a year. She still has some of that left in her savings.

Step 3. Ali worked out really early on that she was running a business

Yes, you are a coach, maybe an author, maybe a course deliverer. You are also now an entrepreneur and that means that you are running a business. So many coaches don't even think about the business side of running their practice.

You have to put a great deal in place from the start if your business is going to run smoothly and survive. To help others starting out Ali has written a book on this (the book she wishes she had when she started out) with her fellow coach Susan Lane, called **'Love Coaching, Hate Business'**, *Simple Steps to Building a Solid Business Foundation for your Coaching Practice. So you can focus on what makes you money.*

In the book they take you through everything you need to consider when starting and running your coaching business:

a) Assess your Entrepreneurship (you da boss!)

b) Nailing your Niche (target practice)

c) Visibility in your marketplace (get seen)

d) Do the Math (show me the money)

e) Plan for Success (you gotta have one)

f) Business Operations (the icky admin stuff)

g) Equipment and Software (stuff you gotta get)

h) The Business of Business (clients and stuff)

i) Website (where the interaction happens)

j) Marketing & Distribution (get out there)

k) LAUNCH YOUR BUSINESS

l) Next Steps: Planning For Growth

m) Final Words: Tips for Success

n) Extra Notes Pages for You

o) About The Authors

p) Recommended Further Reading

q) Business We Recommend

You can order your copy here:
https://www.amazon.co.uk/dp/B09CRH7GJT

Step 4. She nailed down her niche

You cannot overstress how important this is for getting clients, saving time and saving / making money. Your niche is your corner of the marketplace and it's where your ideal client hangs out. You need to be seen and heard there, consistently and with value.

In her book, **'Nailing Your Niche'**, Ali takes you through a proven 5 step process to identify your ideal client, understand what they need that you can offer, how it will benefit them and how you can demonstrate that in your communications.

Get your copy here: https://www.amazon.co.uk/dp/B08LNPTD7X

Step 5. She went hunting.

Not to kill, but to capture.

Having worked out what she does as a coach, who she can help and where they 'hang out' she started targeting her networking and communications. She joined the right Facebook groups, LinkedIn groups, networking groups and Instagram pages in order to connect with and spread her message to her ideal clients. It took time, and effort and a structured plan of action but guess what happened.

She started meeting people who related to her, saw the value in what she was doing and wanted to come and work with her. Sometimes as clients, sometimes as course attendees, sometimes to collaborate on projects with her and sometimes just to buy her books.

Step 6. She grabs every opportunity, and she follows up

Listen, learn, identify where you can make a difference and shout up. It is very true, 'if you don't ask, you don't get', so ask. Put yourself out there. Let's give you an example:

Ali met Marco Bertagni in a breakout room on a networking group.

He talked about his business, and she was intrigued, she talked about her business, and he was intrigued. They were in that room for ten minutes. She could have left it there, but she didn't.

She followed up. Ali contacted Marco, they arranged a zoom call, and they talked and talked and talked, in fact they haven't really stopped talking since then and she quickly became the Director of Business for EMME, 'Eliciting, Mapping and Managing Emotions'. (More about this later).

And she has lost count of the further opportunities that she has 'grabbed' since making that one connection.

What do you learn here?

- You have to believe in yourself wholeheartedly
- Your practice is a business as well as a calling
- It takes time and hard work to get going
- It takes resilience and hard work to keep going
- You need to have the business stuff in place
- You have to know your niche and your ideal client
- You need to target your efforts, and
- You need to go hunting

She is Ali Bagley

Author and / or co-Author of seven business support books
Deliverer of multiple one to many courses on business support and business writing
Business Impact and Writers Coach
Master Geographer of Emotions
Business Director – Emotional Geography UK Ltd

And she is Living her very best life

The Lighthouse of Significance and Growth

As Ali tells it . . .

That chat room, where we met in October 2020, is our **Lighthouse of Significance and Growth**.

We were both, as it turned out, at a crossroads in our individual businesses and looking for (even if we didn't know it then) something that would ramp everything up.

Ali Bagley Coaching was beginning to become established, but I was a bit unfocused and not sure of my next steps. EMME was at a bit of a standstill due to Covid as services had previously been carried out live and Covid had ended that.

I saw in Marco someone who had a methodology that would really help my business and my clients, Marco saw in me someone who could re-design EMME as a growing business in the on-line space and beyond.

And we clicked, we liked each other and felt a great connection. In the months since we met there have been so many weird connections. His first holiday abroad was to the UK, mine was to Italy. We were both born in 1964. Plus, many smaller, yet to us significant connections.

Over the next few months after that first meeting, we began working together to grow EMME, and then redesign and relaunch it as Emotional Geography.

Marco is your typical Italian, romantic, talks a lot, and has big dreams and he is also super intellectual. I am very English, organised, to the point, and cautiously optimistic and I am also super creative.

Because of both our differences and our similar philosophy and moral compasses we found that we complimented each other well. I got on with the practical business stuff, Marco focused on the plans and dreams. I helped Marco to focus his plans and dreams on realistic expectations and he helped me to dream bigger.

When you look at our joint map on page 51 you can see some of our journey for yourself. Make of it what you will, Emotional Geography is very much about personal interpretation.

Suffice to say, we have become great friends who work well together and from that we have built a successful business, with your significance and growth at its heart.

When we finally met, face to face in October 2021 it was like we had known each other forever. In those two weeks in Italy, in between eating, laughing, insulting each other, walking on the beach and drinking good wine and grappa, the dream of the Festival of Emotions began to take shape.

A platform where individuals, groups and organisations could come to meet us, see what we are about, meet our Geographers and from there invest in their future with the courses, journeys and games they would find in the Halls.

The Festival of Emotions is the future of Emotional Geography, and we invite you to visit, to join our community and hopefully, like us, make the connections that will make a positive and significant difference to your personal and professional life.

THE FLOW OF THE RIVER

OUR MAP

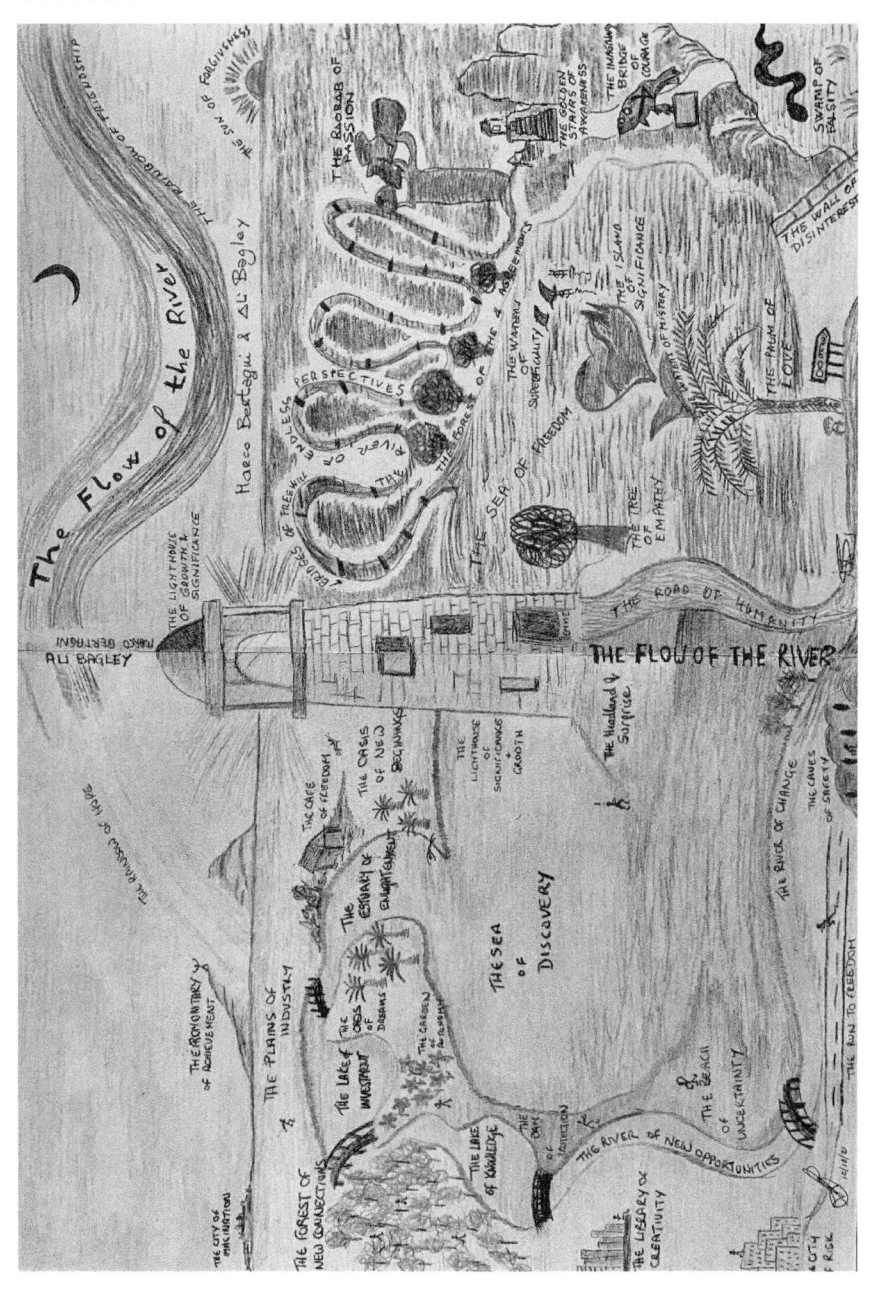

As Marco tells it . . .

Who would have said that *that* chat room, where Ali and I met in October 2020, was going to be a sliding door!? I saw this lady in her office, with many objects around, without by this meaning anything, although I am quite minimalist.

I frankly don't remember what the topic was about, but I perfectly have in mind my first thought about Ali: 'Marco get her contacts and have a talk with her'. Luckily, she did not skip this Latin invitation! We had this talk, and it was like we had known each other for ages! The second thing I thought about Ali – well, the third if we count the "many objects" consideration – was "This Lady Makes The Difference"!

I was dramatically correct! We started seeing each other on an average of 2 hours per day (but she doesn't even realise this since time flies for her when she's with me). She goes on speaking her mysterious Lichfield English without caring about the extraordinary efforts in terms of the focus I need to understand her each time!

This path of growth with Ali was not only connected to improving my English. It was connected to sooo many other things. The River of Life project and EMME – after 5 years of growth and the delivery of more than 100 events – was then ready for upgrading. For a considered jump into other dimensions. And I had it clear from the very beginning that Ali could be the person to deeply help me in this further growth of EMME.

Since we met, we have got along so well together having fun, talking seriously, planning, exchanging views (to finally understand that the Italian was almost always right), we realised many things.

It was the perfect STORM! Or better said the perfect BRAIN STORM, where I was the brain and Ali the storm! I love making fun of her because she thinks I am joking [but I am serious]. Well, Ali is now my deputy director at Bertagni Consulting srl and involved in all the areas of the Company: not only Training and Education – now run through EMME-Emotional Geography UK Ltd – but also International Trading and Corporate Lobbying.

What I love most about her is her sense of organization and the fact that she's positive, optimistic and loyal.

She's hard worker and loves what she does. And so do I: we totally agree on no borders between personal life and professional life. It is just LIFE, and it deserves to be lived at its best.

Which is what Ali and I want to do; share this concept with the many friends who already and have yet to join us in our mission of a better world of respect for self, others and the world!

THE FLOW OF THE RIVER

CHAPTER 3: THE METHODOLOGY

The History of Geo-Emotional Mapping (GEM)

Geo-Emotional Mapping is not new.

How we use it as a methodology is new and unique to EMME.

However, people have been creating these maps for centuries.

The first map of significance was drawn by Madeleine de Scudéry in the 17th century.

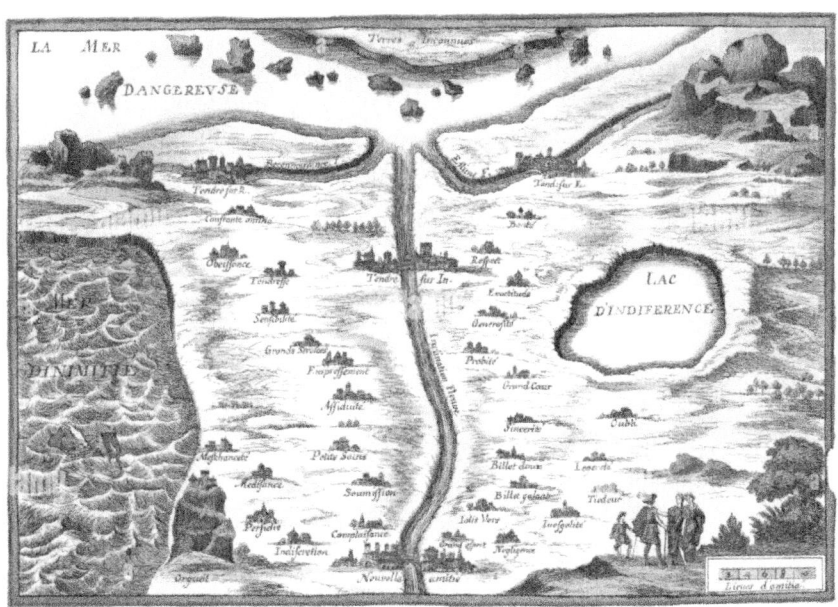

She was a writer, who often published her work under her

brother's name. In her 94 years she produced many books, including: **Artamène, ou le Grand Cyrus** (10 vols., 1648–53), **Clélie** (10 vols., 1654–61), **Ibrahim, ou l'illustre Bassa** (4 vols., 1641), **Almahide, ou l'esclave reine** (8 vols., 1661–63) which were the delight of Europe, yet we would consider them to be very heavy tomes today.

In **Clélie**, Scudéry invented the famous Carte de Tendre **that you see above**, a map of an Arcadia where the geography is all based around the theme of love: the river of Inclination flows past the villages of "Billet Doux" (love letter), "Petits Soins" (Little Trinkets) and so forth.

Marco did his Geography doctorate on the History of Emotional Cartography (at the University of Rome) starting from the analysis of The Map of Tender by Madeleine de Scudéry, and then moving on to the applications and history of the subject.

City planners have used Geo-Emotional Mapping for community development for some years. The process involves pairing a positive response with overall feelings regarding a particular area, building appeal, the usage of green space, location of conveniences, etc. helping to design a more pleasing environment.

Over the last few hundred years examples of Geo-Emotional maps have been seen now and again yet it is only now that we are beginning to see their true value, especially in relation to our mental wellbeing and as a tool for our personal and professional growth.

Traditional Timeline Coaching v's GEM

Timeline coaching is based on using the 'temporal' and 'spatial' sub-modalities. All of our experiences are 'encoded' in our unconscious mind and our UNCONSCIOUS mind can find those, even if our conscious mind can't. Bear in mind that in a coaching clients mind, some events may have been shielded to 'protect' them.

Primarily we use Timeline to release and deal with negative emotions. The coach role is to facilitate the client in releasing negative emotions stemming from a single 'root-cause' event or chain of events; a negative emotion that may be preventing them from achieving their desired goals.

Negative emotions can include, but are not limited to:

Fear   Anger   Lack of self-love   Shame   Grief   Regret

Timeline coaching is a verbal / internal methodology that requires the client to clearly create pictures in his or her mind and then analyse them internally. Whilst it has its place, the benefits can only be recorded in the conscious / sub conscious mind and as such may be short lived. Furthermore, for the client who finds it difficult to create images in their mind this is not a great technique as without the pictures, timeline coaching struggles to be effective in any meaningful or lasting way.

With Geo-Emotional Mapping we lift the imagery out of the mind onto the paper. In both words and pictures. It doesn't require a hypnotic state to carry out and the results are recorded physically, can be revisited and are easier to analyse.

Plus, with Geo-Emotional Mapping you can visit many emotional events and places in one map drawing session. With Timeline coaching you are limited to a max of one or two events in any one session.

And finally, Timeline coaching is about releasing negative emotions that are holding us back so that we can get past them and move on.

GEM is about identifying both positive and negative emotions so that the client can learn from their success and failure, celebrate wins and move past losses. As a tool it has a far broader reach and thus greater results for the client. It is a whole picture exercise, not a single event one.

Remember, we are more than just individual events, we are the sum of *everything* that has gone before.

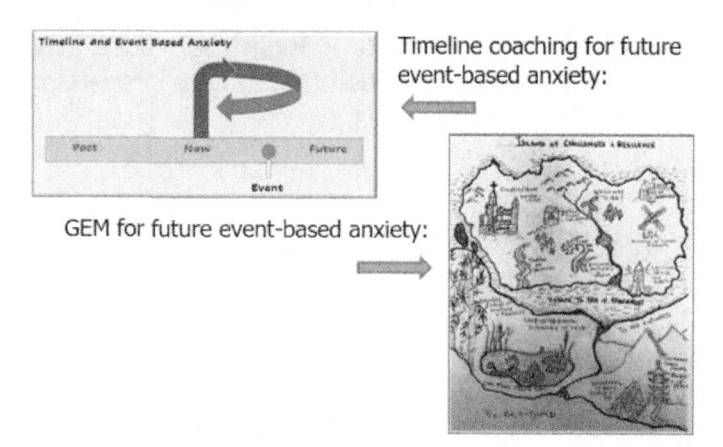

Timeline coaching for future event-based anxiety:

GEM for future event-based anxiety:

Bringing GEM into the 21st Century

Marco, having studied the History of Emotional Cartography and creating his river of life map in 2015, found that he had hit on a way to use that knowledge to develop a methodology for capturing emotions in maps. Not just as pictures or stories, although every map is indeed a story, but as a way for individuals to chart their past present and future in a way that elicits their feelings in a given moment.

By adding the extra element of identifying a geographical feature (hence Geo-emotional mapping) it became easy to step back and see so much information in a map, and from a detached, third-party point of view.

So why is that so relevant in the 21st Century?

It is estimated that in the world today (according to Mental Health England - https://mhfaengland.org/mhfa-centre/research-and-evaluation/mental-health-statistics/:

- 1 in 4 people experience mental health issues each year
- 792 million people are affected by mental health issues worldwide
- At any given time, 1 in 6 working-age adults have symptoms associated with mental ill health

Social media, job pressure, financial worries, the pandemic, these are just a few of the many reasons why people suffer from poor mental health right now. At the same time healthcare funding is stretched to the limit because of the pandemic.

GEM as a methodology is cheap, simple to use and once learned can be applied across so many different circumstances, scenarios, projects and relationships. At its heart is the fact that once you have drawn your geo-emotional map you become more self-aware, more able to identify your strengths, understand your weaknesses, see the tools you have to overcome threats and grow your confidence to help you to take advantage of opportunities.

By doing this life gets better. When life gets better, mental health issues have a chance to diminish.

How Geo-Emotional Mapping Works

The Methodology

Metaphorically speaking we all travel along our own river of life. How often do we stop to look at the map of our journey? How do we capture it?

Geo-emotional mapping enables us to graphically capture our journey through our past, establish where we are now and plot a course for our future.

There is a methodology, a process for mapping, however there are no rules. Every individual is the expert in their own life. Therefore, how you draw your map, where you start, where you end, all of that is up to the cartographer. Of course, every map follows a river, the River of Life.

We choose a place to start, a real place that we associate with our earliest memories. Maybe you choose to begin before you were born, before you knew anything, a place where you were waiting or living another life.

Wherever you plot the starting point on your map it tends to be either at the source of the river or the sea.

So, we choose our starting point. Then we associate that place with how we felt at that time, our emotional state. We then move from reality to imagination and give the real place a new name, based on geological features, astral aspects, weather phenomenon or structures.

For example.

Ali might choose Bristol in the UK as her starting point as that is where she was born. It is on the estuary of the river Avon so likely she will begin at the sea and work back up the river to the source.

She doesn't remember being born but as she moves to imagination, she might see a sunrise, a new beginning. She feels aware, she is born, she lives.

So, she names this starting point on her River of Life 'the Sunrise of Awareness'. And she draws my interpretation of the sunrise.

As you can see, no artistic talent is required!

In this way you continue to plot the key events of your life along the river, sometimes stepping onto the bank, maybe taking a diversion along a tributary, but always coming back to the flow of the river.

The Wheels

To help you on your journey we suggest some geographical places, phenomena and features for you along with different emotional states you might experience. We do this in two wheels. Again, no rules, make up your own places and emotions. Whatever works for you.

The key here is to both visualise a place in your mind's eye and really take notice of your emotions, how you feel in that moment in time.

We travel through our past, into our present and onto our future, and beyond. Thus, we create the geo-emotional map of our River of Life.

Once your map is draw comes the analysis stage. That is very subjective, personal to each individual and has enormous power when it is shared with others, as in the Map Out Your Emotions workshops we run for people who are new to GEM.

THE FLOW OF THE RIVER

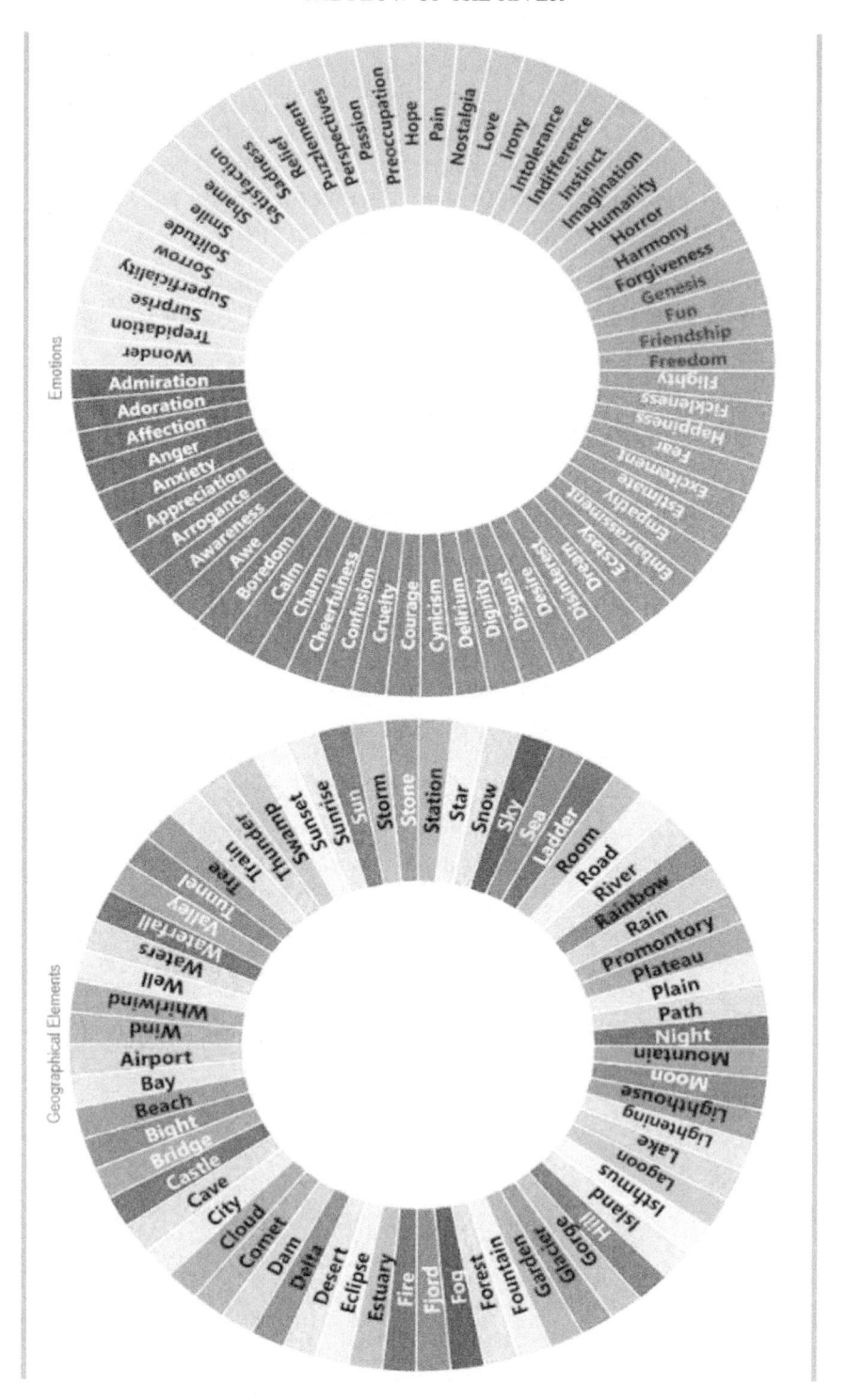

The Importance of Travel

Travel plays a key role in The River of Life.

Travel inside of ourselves to learn about our emotions, our values, our beliefs and our talents.

Travel to new places, physically or metaphysically, gaining new experiences, learning about other cultures and increasing our knowledge of the world.

Travel beyond your own boundaries and expanding your horizons through learning new skills and new information.

We are constantly moving and growing and changing as we travel the River of Life. Always in the hope of a brighter future for ourselves, those we care for and those friends we have not yet met.

In Chapter 5, 'Fearless' you will see how to fully use Emotional Geography as a methodology for your Growth and Significance. What follows in this chapter is an overview of how we map in our sessions and what we get from that.

Your Map

Just letting your imagination run free as you draw your map is cathartic in itself. What you then learn as you step away from your map and then look back at it is very often astounding.

No matter how well or badly drawn, no matter how confusing it might appear to others, you will know exactly what it is about, will be able to discover so much from it and use it to make the positive changes you need to.

Look at the maps we shared in the Introduction, complete nonsense to the casual observer, life changing for the cartographers. But the real power, the thing that takes this one step nearer to life changing, is the sharing.

The Sharing

Because your map gives you a third-party perspective on your journey it is so much easier to tell your story than if you were say, in a one-to-one coaching session and were asked to simply describe your journey in words.

Talking about your past, and often your hopes for the future, is often a very emotional experience and can be difficult, particularly if you have faced many obstacles and challenges.

What we have discovered, is that when you share your map, in other words tell the story of your journey by recounting what you see draw there, not only do you learn more than you would just by looking at it alone, but also you can gain much more perspective and objectivity about those events.

And you also help the others listening. Believe me you are never the only one who has gone through a bad situation and the shared support that we see in readings is immense.

The Discoveries

Discoveries differ from map to map, person to person. Here are a selection of things that your map might help you to discover:

- You have survived everything that has gone before
- Even when things get really bad they always get better
- Your particular skills and expertise
- Your triggers and temptations
- Your coping methods
- Your happy place
- What to do next
- What you really want from life
- What you don't want from life!
- Things you should avoid
- Things you should embrace
- Who you really are

And that is just the tip of the iceberg!

Pack Your Luggage

This a game, the first of the two key games developed to introduce you to the methodology of Geo-emotional Mapping. In it you will first 'unpack' your emotional baggage and then 'repack' to arm yourself with the mental attributes that will serve you on your life's journey.

Time to Draw Your Geo-Emotional River of Life Map

Once we have packed our luggage we move on to 'Map Out Your Emotions', the second of the two key games. In this interactive session you will learn how to draw your map and to do an initial analysis so that you can use it to plan forward.

Analysis

Time Distribution

First, we divide the map into past, present and future.

Physical Geography and Place Symbolism

Then we look at why you have made the symbolic choices you have made in creating your map. You can attach meanings and learnings to this symbolism.

Sharing

The last but some say the most impactful part of the game, sharing your map, and so your story, with others. It can be very emotional, sometimes difficult to do but in every case, we see people learning and growing and becoming stronger.

THE FLOW OF THE RIVER

CHAPTER 4: SEEING THINGS FROM ANOTHER PERSPECTIVE, UNLOCKING THE SECRETS IN YOUR MAP

Self-Awareness

In order to grow and become more significant as an individual, both in your personal and professional life, self-awareness is vitally important. After all, if we do not know ourselves how can we work out what needs to change and how to do it?

Self-awareness is the core of Geo-emotional Mapping. By drawing, sharing and analysing your map you are able to take a step out of yourself and look back in from a third-party perspective. In fact, this actually serves to disassociate you from yourself and so be less emotionally involved.

Third-Party Perception

Taking that detached viewpoint enables you to be more subjective, arguably more honest with yourself and for sure more able to gain clarity about the situation / challenge / relationship / life that you have mapped.

It's like you become your own best friend, able to see things from another's point of view and so then able to give better advice.

Highlighting the Positives

Begin by noting all the challenges you have overcome. How did you do it, how did you feel, where might those skills or actions be useful to you again.

Know that you are the survivor of all that has gone before.

Then look at the times where you have not succeeded or have struggled. This too is positive because from that you can learn what not to do again and what doesn't work *for you*.

Creating Your In-Depth Breakdown

In the chapter Fearless we give you an overview of the things you can do to create an in-depth analysis of any map you draw.

We recommend you buy the full book 'Fearless' which is available as a downloadable pdf here: https://alibagleycoach.samcart.com/products/fearless---a-geography-through-the-geography-of-emotions for just £3.99

Creating Your Action Plan for Success

Geo-Emotional Mapping is fun, especially when it is done as part of a game or a metaphysical journey and so you may want to learn about it just for that.

Most of you will want to be able to use it as a tool to make a difference in your life. To understand yourself better, to work out what you want in life or a given situation, maybe even to work out which direction to take next.

The thing is, you are going to get a lot of data about yourself and your situation from your mapping, but unless you use that data it is just that, data.

Once you have created your map and you have your data, the way that it will help you to make the positive changes you want is to use it to create a plan of action.

Plan of Action = Your directions to navigate your way through the future part of your map in order to get you to your desired location.

You will know what you want to achieve, the plan is all about how you do it.

The next chapter is going to help you with that.

THE FLOW OF THE RIVER

CHAPTER 5: FEARLESS - GETTING CLOSER TO YOUR AMBITIONS AND DREAMS

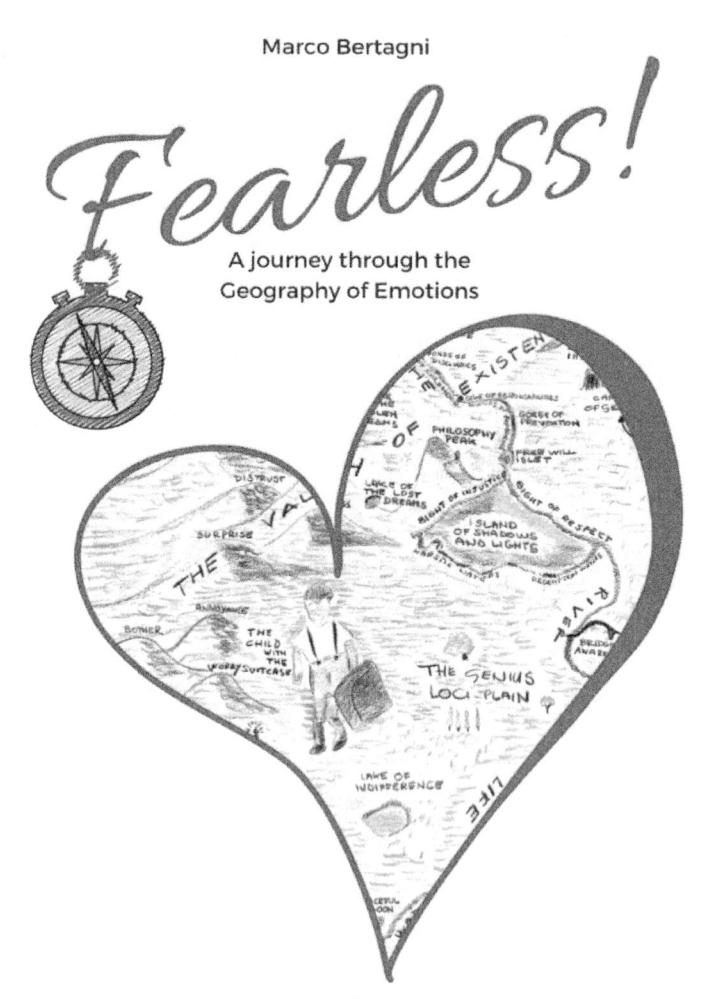

Marco Bertagni

Fearless!

A journey through the Geography of Emotions

GUIDELINES TO EXPLORE YOUR OWN RIVER OF LIFE
IN SEARCH OF A NEW AWARENESS

Taking inspiration from the book THE RIVER OF LIFE (Editions Associazione Lorenzo Guarnieri, 2016), Marco Bertagni now presents us his journey into the geography of emotions in the form of an workbook, sharing the tools that enabled him to embark on a personal path of growth and discovery.

The author urges everyone to nake their soul, to (re)find their emotions, to pull them out to embark on a journey that approaches us with a serene and multi-prospective perception of Ourselves, the Others and the World.

Tell us fearless about these emotions! Each of us has a beautiful story to tell.

To ourselves first and then to those who have a great quality: being able to listening to others.

We move the first step of a path of self-awareness and re-vision of the world we live in. We return to the core of what is really important to the human being, abandon the surface, and especially the superficiality, for the lightness and serching depth instead of heaviness.

Love for life, this is, perhaps, the only secret!

Good trip and ... become who you are!

The journey, a deep emotion.

THE RIVER OF LIFE PROJECT
theriveroflife.it

From the River of Life to "Fearless"

To come across a picture, that his Aunt Diana told him about for years, was, for Marco Bertagni the trigger of a journey through the geography of emotions and the beginning of a *rational dream* called THE RIVER OF LIFE.

The visual impact with his soul, with his essence, with his spirit, the irrefutable perception of his existential vocation (the journey), that amused and dreamy smile, the familiarity and closeness he felt towards the inner world of that child 50 years after the picture was taken: all these were very strong emotions!

To find that picture was some sort of key-moment, and, in the following months, he began to feel, with increasing strength, the desire to identify, to pull out, and to confront his most significant, most rooted and most indelible emotions, the deepest states of mind, his dreams, his ways to look at and to face the World.

And so he did, without restraint, without fear, until he found himself in a kind of emotional maelstrom, wrapped by intense feelings.

The next step was to try to give an order to this chaos. Almost instinctively, in September 2015, he started drawing a map, an itinerary to recommend to the child with the suitcase who was actually embarking on his emotional journey, but who was occasionally a bit...disoriented.

Fifty imaginary places, starting in the Canyon of Genesis and ending in the Sea of Freedom.

The child began to project his moods, his fantasies, his experiences on every single imaginary place. At the same time, he thought about real geographies, physical places that evoked the emotions to which that imaginary place on the map was referring.

In the same way, while travelling, music, works of art, emotional objects came to his mind and helped him get to the top of the Peak of Joy or on the shores of the Lake of Lost Dreams, in the presence of the imposing Dike of Responsibilities or in the intriguing Island of Perspectives.

He dreamed, he laughed, he cried. He took possession of and then released his own emotions.

A different child came out - as you make your way by going – a better child, a more serene, more conscious, less frantic one.

These are at least the feelings that he, (raised) child with the suitcase, felt at the end of this journey.

Finally, Marco converged these reasoned passions or passionate reasonings in a book, published by Association Lorenzo Guarnieri in 2016 and entitled THE RIVER OF LIFE. Here, by means of the artistic forms that he feels closer to him, namely writing and photography, he tried to translate into words and images the journey he had just taken by following the emotional map.

From that moment on, what was a private journey in his initial intentions has slowly turned into a kind of paradigmatic itinerary that seems to somehow stimulate the mapping of personal versions of THE RIVER OF LIFE.

It is in this context that the workbook FEARLESS! comes into play.

By means of this book, that enforces and is inspired by THE RIVER OF LIFE, Marco would like to share the logical-emotional tools and passages that helped him embark on this path of growth and self-awareness.

To build and to explore your own River of Life means to get back to the substance, to the soul of things, of places, of people, and of yourself.

He therefore invites you, dear reader, to perceive, to "listen", with all your senses, to the River flowing in the Valley of Existence: its smells, its sometimes calm sometimes forceful mòtŭs, its geographies, its colours, the creatures filling up its shores and its waters, its traps, its imperturbability, its strength to change and to remain itself at the same time.

Yes... the mōtŭs: according to the Latin, it means movement, passion, feeling, sensation, activity of the spirit, emotion of the soul. The two concepts, motion and emotion, are symbiotic. Marco believes that life - as a flowing river – must be in motion, but to stop and to listen to that river can sometimes be healthy.

FEARLESS! - at the end - wants to be just this: a reminder to live...your life.

It is a moment of reflection on the water that flowed, that is now flowing and that will flow in our River, on the water that evaporates and goes to heaven and on the water that heaven gives us back.

Let's sit on a rock on the riverbank in a convinced effort to regain the emotions - that we often push away and that are altered or separated from us -, to follow our vocations, to feel the spirit of the places, to approach our own soul and that of the world.

So, from now on try to connect your geo-emotional dots and then create the mosaic of your life in the forms of expression that you feel closer to your being. Each of us has talents. Each of us has a story that is worth telling. And being listened to.

Bare your soul. FEARLESS!

Raise the sails to the wind and set sail!

The departure, a deep emotion.

Fearless is available in pdf from the Shop at www.emotional-geography.com or directly from here: https://alibagleycoach.samcart.com/products/fearless---a-geography-through-the-geography-of-emotions

The Paperback will be available on Amazon soon.

THE FLOW OF THE RIVER

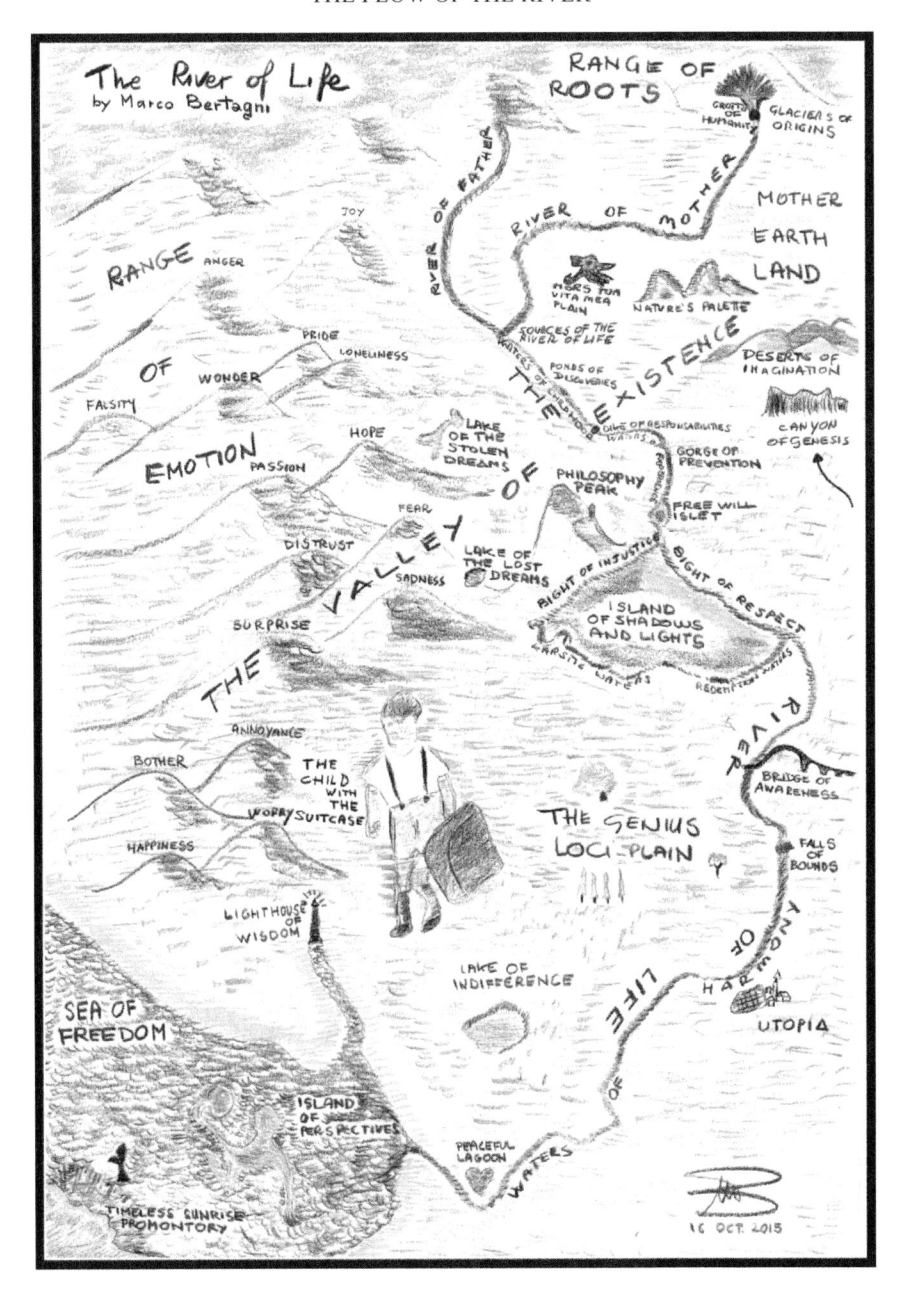

THE TASTE OF GEO-EMOTIONS

One of the many applications of THE RIVER OF LIFE

FEARLESS! Is a sort of prequel of **THE RIVER OF LIFE** while **THE TASTE OF GEO-EMOTIONS** could be considered a sequel or an application – among many others – of Marco's journey through emotional geography.

The book **THE TAST OF GEO-EMOTIONS**, stems from long summer discussions between the co-authors Marco Bertagni and Giuseppe Bertoli, about philosophy, emotions and - like good Italians - food and drink, obviously. These topics have not been tackled in the abstract, but by keeping in mind the geo-emotional map of The River of Life.

Since Marco first told him about The River of Life, Giuseppe showed a great interest and curiosity and he bombarded Marco with questions, also and above all, about the pictures of the book.

Marco noticed that Giuseppe tried to "listen" to the book, to perceive its several messages and narrative forms.

Then one day, suddenly Giuseppe told Marco that he had thought of a dish to match with the picture of Marco at 3 with the suitcase and he described Marco the shape and the ingredients: a puff pastry in the shape of a dumpling, (the symbol of the ancient travellers), lying on mushy peas (green as the colour of hope that is inherent in every journey) and wrapped in a yoghurt, white as the symbol of the purity of each beginning).

He added that he would have identified this dish with the River of Father, one of the emotional places of the ROOTS stage, because, according to him, Marco the father of this project and also the person that has made him understand the real reason for his being cook: the capability to be moved, that gastronomic creation can give him.

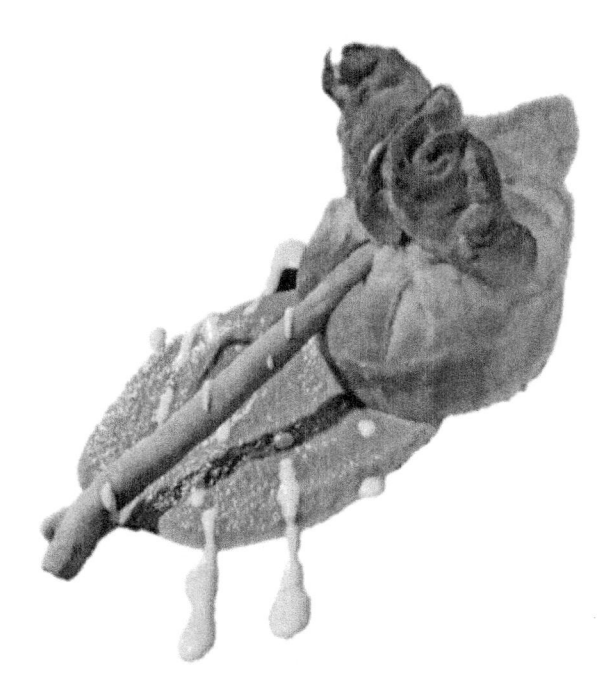

And from that moment on, it was all a sharing of life events, memories, dreams, trying to connect everything to one or more emotional places or real one.

Then, it was but a short step from that first connection child with the suitcase - herbal ricotta dumpling on mushy peas and yoghurt - River of Father to the next one Giuseppe as a child who played on the banks of Serchio while his father went fishing and smoked a cigar - trout dessert - Waters of Childhood, and so on until we created 50 recipes, one for each emotional place of the map.

But maybe we just re-created recipes on the basis of personal direct emotions, the ones originated from the pictures of the book, the ones symbolised by the imaginary geography of The River of Life map, or on the basis of the feelings arising from the real geography of Garfagnana (The Valley of Existence) and Serchio (The River of Life), but also Polesine (The River of Mother), Portugal (Waters of Harmony) and Anzio (Sea of Freedom).

In the book, Chef Giuseppe Bertoli provides the ingredient list for each recipe, describes it and shows a picture of the gastronomic creation.

In each chapter, for those recipes that provoked the Chef the deepest emotions, an explanation of the geo-emotional origin is provided: the background.

These top-emotional recipes are complemented by a picture, that is taken from the book The River of Life and is related to the emotional place coupled with that particular recipe.

A recapitulative synoptic table has been included after the description of individual recipes.

The last part of the book deals with the interaction with the reader.

On the one hand, the reader is asked to match the 50 imaginary places of the emotional map with 50 dishes and beverages (which were enjoyed during his/her life in as many real places), through the use of a matrix. In this way, a personal geographic, wine and gastronomic river will be built.

On the other hand, the reader is requested to build his/her own The River of Life menu, by "creating" a dish for each stage of the journey (Earth, Roots, Emotions, Life, Philosophy and Freedom), and to match each dish with the 50 emotional places of the map.

We suggest creating 6 complementary dishes (starter, main course 1, main course 2, second course, dessert, fruit) that, if aggregated, can represent your original geo-emotional lunch (or dinner) proposal.

There is a story to tell, the story of your River of Life.

In this book, you will find the instructions to identify, pull out and represent your emotions through the cooking.

We will trace together a tasty emotional map.

The Taste of Geo-emotions is available in pdf here:
https://alibagleycoach.samcart.com/products/the-taste-of-geo-emotions---e-book

THE FLOW OF THE RIVER

CHAPTER 6: PROBLEM SOLVING - DIFFERENT APPLICATIONS FOR GEO-EMOTIONAL MAPPING

Overview

What situations, circumstances, challenges can you use Geo-Emotional Mapping to better understand? Honestly, many, many, many. Here we talk about just a few:

- Life
- Business
- Career
- Relationships
- Health
- Recovery
- Legacy
- Family
- Travel
- Storytelling
- Project Management
- Team Building
- Fun and Games

Over the next pages you will see a selection of geo-emotional maps, drawn by ourselves and our clients, mostly in shared mapping experiences.

These maps show you the diversity of situations in which geo-emotional mapping can be used effectively as a tool for self-awareness and growth.

For Life

Most of us start our journey with Geo-Emotional Mapping by creating our River of Life Map. This is a map that charts our whole life, from the past, into now and onto the future.

This mapping enables us to better understand who we are, what we really want from life as a whole and what we have learned so far to help us to have better lives in the future. This is the map you will create when you join one of our live **Map out Your Emotions** sessions.

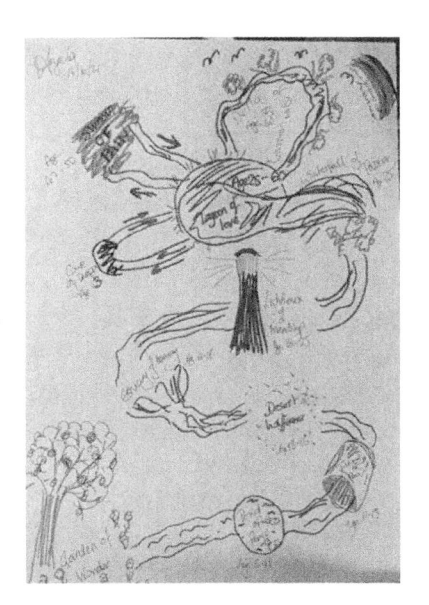

For Business

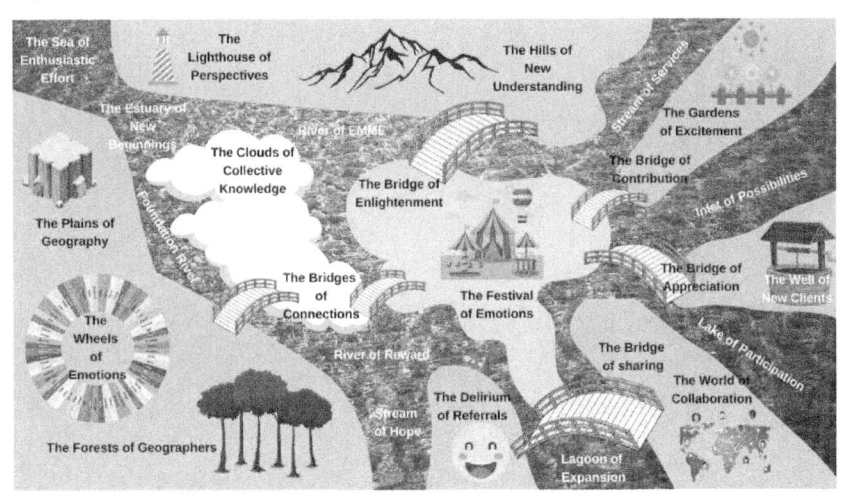

Creating a map of your business can make things so much clearer for you. It identifies your challenges, helps you to learn from past success, identifies gaps in skills and knowledge, and helps you to plan a strategy to move your business forward.

It is great for creating clarity from chaos in terms of where your business is heading and how to get it to where you want it to be.

For Career

Not happy in your current job? Not sure what you want to do in the future? Unsure of your strengths and weaknesses? Know what you want but unsure how to get it?

These are all questions that mapping out the river of your career can answer for you, as well as helping you to plan the actions you need to take to get to where you want to be.

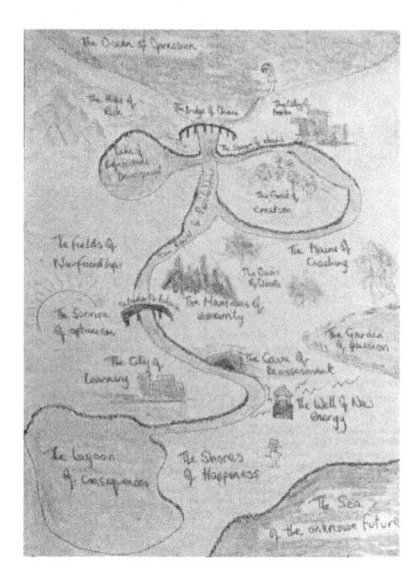

For Relationships

Single but not sure what you want in a partner? In a relationship but unhappy? Recovering from a break-up?

Make a map of your past relationships, where you are now and what is important to you. That will really clarify things for you and help you to make a plan to get what you want from a relationship or to mend or end one you are already in.

For Health

We use GEM for looking at our emotional relationship with food and how it has led to weight problems, we use it to map out our health journey and see what really works for us and what doesn't. We use it to develop a healthier relationship with ourselves and others.

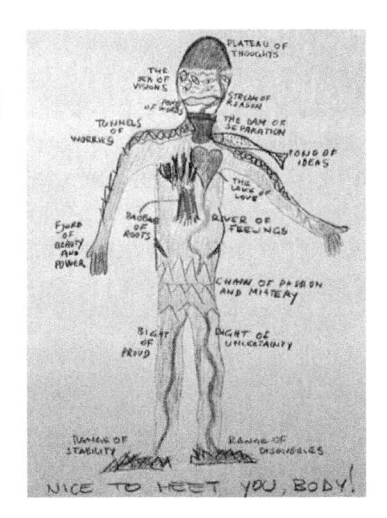

For Legacy

Your River of Life Map is a snapshot of your life for your development and growth. It can also be used to create a legacy for your loved ones. Creating a map that details the path of your life, your happiness, your struggles, your triumphs, pivotal events like the birth of your children or the loss of your parents. This can be a beautiful gift to leave as a legacy.

For Recovery

There are many types of trauma; abuse, PTSD, broken relationships, grief, depression and anxiety. GEM can be used to map out that trauma and learn about you, your relationship with the trauma, the impact it has had on you and how to manage it going forward.

For Family

Family relationships can be fraught with challenges and also provide the most joyful moments. Understanding your family, close and extended, can be multi-layered and difficult. GEM can help you to separate those layers and get to the heart of what you want from your family relationships and how to do it.

For Travel

Why not create a Geo-Emotional Map next time you go on holiday to capture the events from each day? It will give you a fabulous souvenir, and as you do more and more, will build into a record of all your trips.

We also use GEM in our Metaphysical Journeys, where we travel virtually to a place and working in teams, create a story told using the maps we create.

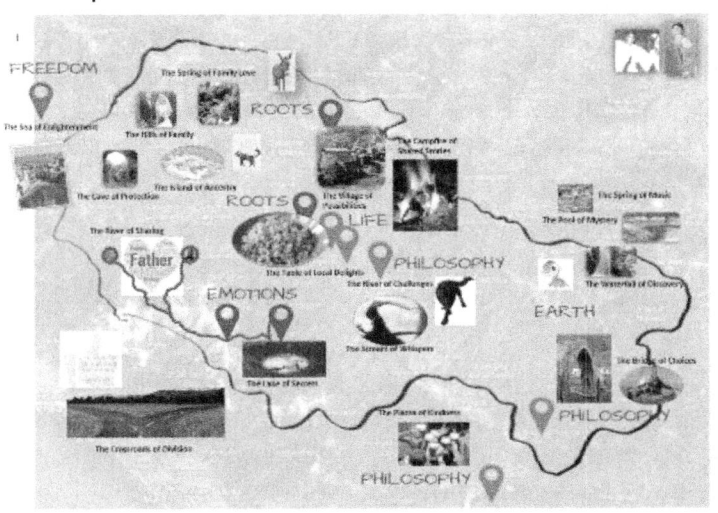

For Storytelling, Book Writing and Scripts

Creatives, this is for you. GEM is brilliant as a methodology for planning out any story you want to sell, everything from developing a marketing campaign to writing a novel, to writing a movie script.

You can plot your story along the river of the project and see it much more clearly than when you capture it on a thousand post it notes or in multiple word documents on your laptop.

For Project Analysis

Using GEM for project management and analysis is another way to see things from another point of view. Get your team to each talk a stakeholder role and map how they see the project developing from that stakeholders' point of view. Then have a round table discussion. You will be amazed at how this makes for better project delivery as well as better team working.

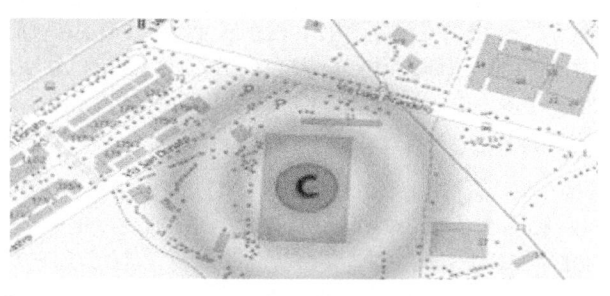

We offer bespoke facilitation of these sessions for your team. Just contact Ali or Marco for more details.

For Team Building

As with Projects above, using GEM in your teams to tackle a problem or just see things from different points of view works brilliantly in bringing teams together, identifying each individuals' strengths and weaknesses and getting solutions to issues.

For Fun and Games

Last but not least, let's have some fun. We have developed many games using geo-emotional mapping techniques for businesses, individuals and teams. Most can be done virtually, and all can be incorporated into bespoke packages for organisations for team building, skills development and project management.

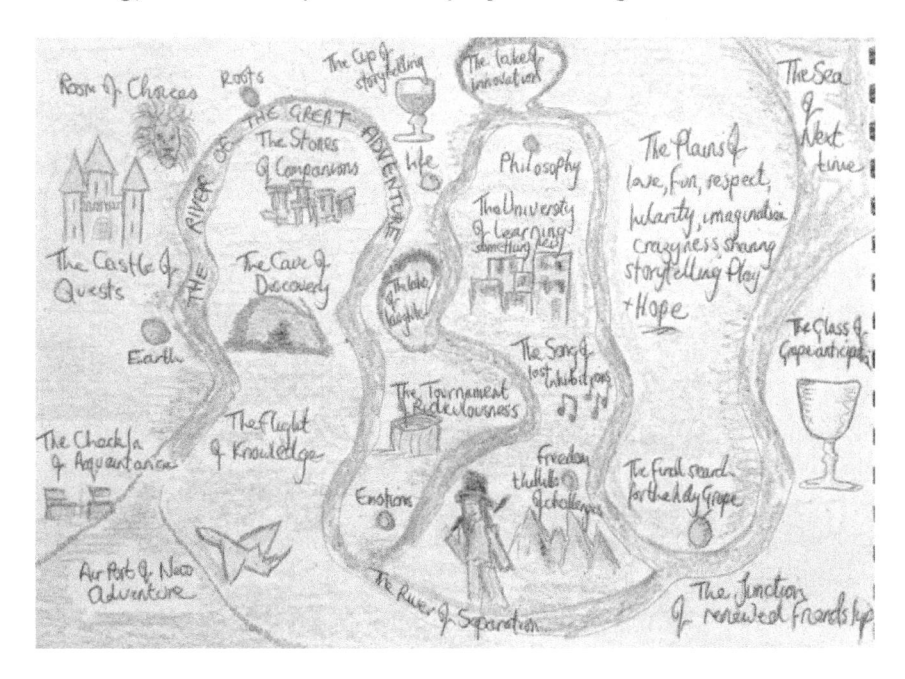

THE FLOW OF THE RIVER

CHAPTER 7: BUILDING A COMMUNITY

EMME – The Community

We told you a bit about us in Chapter 1. To remind you, we are simply citizens of the world with a thirst for gaining and sharing knowledge who use Geo-Emotional Mapping as a tool for our growth and significance.

We are from all over the world and so we mostly meet virtually through zoom although when we get the chance to actually be in the same room with others, we grab it.

We meet weekly as the community on a call where we talk about life, challenges, triumphs, what's going on, and sometimes we are just really silly and play a game or swap (really bad) jokes.

We support each other as a network. We lend our skills to each other, we share others news and businesses across our networks, we attend each other's events, and we provide a platform, through the Festival of Emotions, for members of our community to shout out about themselves and what they have to offer.

What We Do

As Geographers of Emotions we use GEM to create courses, journeys and games to help others to learn and grow. To solve problems, to gain clarity, to learn specific new skills, to communicate better and to expand their horizons.

Why We Do It

We are all individuals so why we do it is extremely varied but there are a few commonalities:

- We love to learn and to share what we learn.
- We have seen how powerful GEM is and want others to benefit from it too.
- We enjoy the different opportunities we have in the community to expand our horizons, through events, collaboration, calls, courses, journeys and games.
- We all want to grow as individuals and professionals into the best version of who we are.
- We understand the power of emotions to be both a positive or negative force and we are learning to elicit, map and manage them through GEM

How We Do It

We design, develop and deliver multiple services which fall into the categories of:

Courses – counselling, coaching and consultancy

Journeys – actual (Geo-maieutical) and virtual (metaphysical)

Games – board games and outdoor games

These services can be found in our catalogue which you can download from the Festival of Emotions.

These services are delivered either online as pre-recorded modular courses, on zoom as interactive live sessions or in person, particularly for corporations and educational institutions.

Who We Are

84 (as of 1st January 2022) Geographers of Emotions, several licensees and an online community of 500+ FB group members.

Our FB Group – EMME – Geographers of Emotions – can be joined here: https://www.facebook.com/groups/213734233615058

We come from all over the world. We are coaches, entrepreneurs, students, managers, actors, film directors, doctors, travel guides, trainers, singers, lawyers, nurses, teachers and so much more.

We are many different colours, we speak many different languages, we are from many different cultures, but at heart we are all the same, citizens of the world.

Networking

84 people, all with different skills, capabilities, knowledge and things to offer. We network a lot, on zoom, though the FB group and soon via the forum that will be on the Festival of Emotions website.

Collaboration

Since joining the community we have all made new friends and connections. As a result, people are creating things in collaboration with each other that they would never have had the opportunity to do otherwise.

Marco and Ali have collaborated on many games, journeys and courses and have written two books together. Ali has also created courses with other Geographers. Some have started working outside of the community on projects and in businesses that they have found through networking within the community.

Some have found new clients for their businesses; some have found new business for their needs.

This community is about sharing, getting to know each other, celebrating all that is Geo-Emotional Geography and helping others to achieve growth and significance in their lives.

There are no limits other than those we put upon ourselves. Rivers are free and so are we.

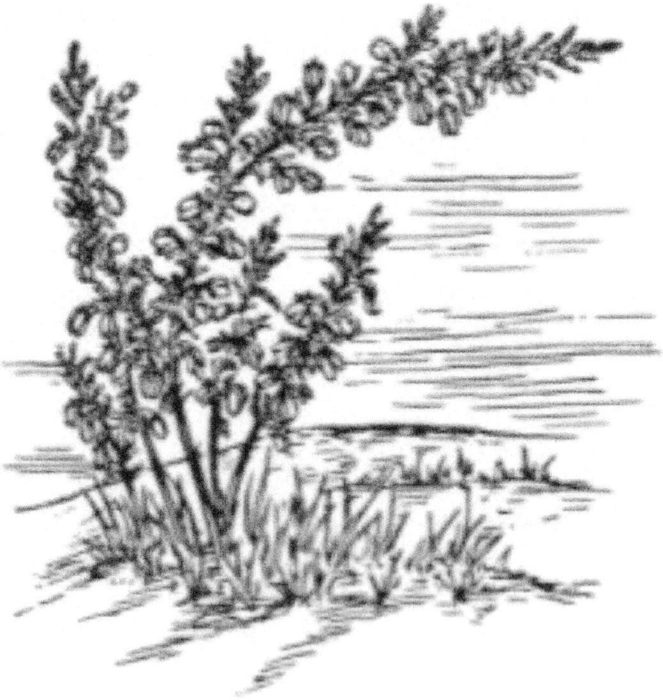

CHAPTER 8: ONE TO ONE OR GROUP GEO-EMOTIONAL MAPPING AS A TOOL TO GROW YOUR BUSINESS

As a Client

We have what you need for . . .

- Team Building
- Project Management
- Sales Training
- Intercultural Working
- International Trading

Our courses, journeys and games can all be delivered to individuals or teams, as stand-alone experiences or as a bespoke package built specifically for your business needs.

The best way to access the benefits for your business is to become a Corporate Member of the Festival of Emotions. As a Corporate Member either Marco or I or one of our team with knowledge of your industry will be appointed as your dedicated Account Manager. What does that mean?

Your Account Manager is going to find out about you and your business and what your people need to drive productivity, output, teamwork etc. forward.

Based on those needs we will develop together a bespoke package of experiences and deliver those, directly to your team, in a way that's suits you, either live, in person or over zoom or as a pre-recorded follow anytime option.

The pricing will be based entirely on the services you want and the number of people we are delivering to and frequency of that delivery. The point here is that everything will be designed specifically for you and your business needs.

Benefits for your people and your business

We build a relationship with you and your business and your people as we get to know you better.

This enables us to continually fine tune our service to you so that you are constantly getting what you really need.

We are not 'off the shelf', we are bespoke. We are also different in that our training, our services, are based in the methodology of geo-emotional mapping. We put the human into human resources. Business is about people, people operate on feelings and emotions, we tap into and make the best of that for you.

Developing Bespoke Training for Your People

Not only will the services we deliver into your business be bespoke to your needs and developed with you, but we also offer train the trainer packages.

This means that you can send one or more of your people to us for our Geographer of Emotions Training. They will then come back to you, complete with license, enable to create your services in house, liaise with us for support and further services and deliver our services into your business.

And as a Corporate Member of the Festival of Emotions you get discounts on that too. Win, win!

Growing Your Business Using Emotional Geography as a tool for your clients

Geo-emotional mapping, as you have seen in the previous chapters is a very powerful tool for coaching and training.

As a coach or trainer, adding this methodology to your toolbox will help you to stand out from your competitors and provide your clients with a more comprehensive service from you.

Becoming a Geographer of Emotions

We currently have 84 Geographers of Emotions. Each year we train and certify a maximum of 40 more. We keep the numbers low because we are a community. To enable us to continually support and nurture our Geographers we need to keep numbers small.

Plus, part of our offer to you is that you will be getting a license to use a methodology that is pretty exclusive.

Training happens four times a year, ten people in each group. The training is delivered online by Ali and Marco over a number of sessions. At the end of the training you will:

- Be able to use Geo-Emotional Mapping confidently and effectively with your clients
- Be able to develop courses, journeys and games using the methodology and get free ongoing support with that
- Have a 1-year renewable license to practice Geo-Emotional Mapping in your business
- Be Certified as a Geographer of Emotions
- Be able to collaborate on developing and delivering services with other Geographers
- Have your bio and services and business featured on the Emotional Geography website – The Festival of Emotions
- Have your Services in the Halls of the Festival of Emotions
- Have your services uploaded to SamCart for sales with all admin done for you and all links back to your services in the Halls
- Sell your books and products in the website shop
- Have free membership of the Festival of Emotions for 1 year
- Be part of an exclusive yet growing community
- Be invited to take part in community events throughout the year
- Have access to Geographer discounts on all of our services

and experiences
- Have the opportunity to progress to Accredited and Master Geographer levels
- Qualify to be a featured Geographer in the Festival.

Becoming a Licensee

Becoming a License is the option for you if you do not want to take advantage of having your services / bio / business highlighted in the Festival of Emotions but do want to use the methodology in your business, either in coaching one to one or in courses you develop independently.

In this case you would do a shorter version of the training which specifically teaches you the methodology and after that you get a free one-year license to use it in your business.

A USP for Your Business

Geo-Emotional Mapping is not only an incredibly powerful tool for developing self-awareness in order to grow and become more significant in your life, but also is a USP for any business based in helping people and organisations to grow and become more significant.

Being able to say that you are a Certified, Accredited or even a Master Geographer of Emotions does a number of things when it comes to your marketing:

1. It sparks interest – 'so what's that then?'
2. It gives you something fairly unique to offer
3. It is backed by a multi-national organisation
4. It is adaptable to the individual needs of your client, individual and corporate
5. It gives you a platform through the community to reach more people and organisations

Using Geo-emotional Geography to Build Your Community

As part of our community as a Geographer of Emotions, a

Licensee, a Festival Member or even as a sponsor / supporter, you will have access to all of our network and the extended network of all of our members.

One of the most fascinating things that have happened in the last year of growing this business is that it has grown organically from those networks, with people joining us from other organisations and networks that we have been involved in. You can take advantage of that when you join our community.

If you want to know more about becoming a Festival Member, Geographer of Emotions, Licensee, Supporter or Sponsor please visit the Festival website at:

https://www.emotional-geography.com

or contact Ali at:

ali@emotional-geography.com

THE FLOW OF THE RIVER

CHAPTER 9: HAVING FUN

Above all else, this community of Geographers of Emotions, Festival Members and Friends, people and having fun is what motivates us, brings us together and makes us what we are.

Yes, providing you with pathways to your growth and significance is what we do, yes, we work hard at that, and we expect our clients to as well, but most of all we want you to leave us with a smile on your face, a spring in your step and a sense of wonder for what is to come.

Actually, we don't want you to leave us, which is why we will continue to provide you with new stuff every week in the Festival of Emotions!

The Journeys

The journeys are for sure where we have the most fun. Both the Live Geo-Maieutical Journeys and the online Metaphysical Journeys are all about people coming together, getting to know each other, tell stories, experience adventures and grow together.

When we plan these journeys, FUN is number one on our list of things to include.

As you can see from the picture above, taken on our first Metaphysical Journey to England, we were having a lot of FUN.

The basic story here . . . we were working as a team and in pairs as we travelled to 6 destinations in England as King Arthurs Knights of the Round Table.

What started as a quest for the Holy Grail soon became a quest for the holy grape, with crazy dragons, lakes of wine, lords and ladies battling it out at tournaments and all kinds of shenanigans.

It was a blast, still talked about weeks later, and we cannot wait to run it again.

All of our Journeys can be found in the Halls of the Festival of Emotions. They take place all over the world and can be designed specifically as team building exercises for your team or organisation, either live or online.

The Community

As a community we like to keep in touch with each other.

Besides the friendships that have been made which go on in the background, we have a bi-weekly networking call where we all meet up.

Originally this call was set up to talk about the business of Emotional Geography, what we were doing, what was coming next etc.

Now it is more like a social event. We have topics to talk around for sure and members are welcome to ask questions, get support and so on, but mostly we just talk about stuff, like you would if you met for a coffee with friends. And there is always laughter.

GEM for Parties and Events

A new service for 2022 which will be launching in the summer is Emotional Geography for parties and events.

Maybe you want to develop a game or journey for your business conference, maybe you want a game for wedding guests at your reception, maybe you are looking for something to entertain guests after a dinner.

We have it all here in the form of ready-made journeys and games but more than that we will create bespoke journeys and games for your event on request.

To find out more contact ali@emotional-geography.com

THE FLOW OF THE RIVER

CHAPTER 10: INSPIRING OTHERS - WHAT IS NEXT FOR US AND FOR YOU

2022 and Beyond

Emotional Geography UK Ltd, the Home of EMME, Eliciting, Mapping and Managing Emotions and where we bring you the Festival of Emotions from is growing.

We have 84 Geographers of Emotions as at the beginning of 2022. We will have well over 100 by the end of the year.

The Festival of Emotions website has been launched, membership starts of 14th March 2022 and every week there will be new content, events, features, offers and competitions to be found there.

For Members of the Festival, you will have access to the Hall of Significance from where you can apply to become a Geographer of Emotions or a Licensee. You will also have access to the Hall of Corporate Collaboration where we can dedicate an Account Manager to your business to work on bespoke services for you.

Members will also have access to the Plaza, where events, news and content specifically for Members can be found.

Of course, you can visit all of the other halls and pages even if you aren't a Member but why would you miss out on all the content, events, discounts and opportunities available by just being a visitor?

The Festival of Emotions

How it Works

As a visitor you can go from the homepage, that tells you about the Festival, to:

- An Introduction from Ali & Marco
- the Geographers of Emotions page
- the Eight Festival Halls Experiences
- The Membership Portal
- News and Announcements
- Download the Catalogue

From the membership Portal, once you have become a Member, you can access the Plaza, The Hall of Significance and the Hall of Corporate Collaboration, plus all of the extra members Only content and events.

What it seeks to Achieve

Emotional Geography needed a home. Somewhere that we could welcome you in, show you around, introduce us to our community and our experiences and provide you with tools for your growth and significance.

The Layout

The Opportunities For Individuals

As an individual we have sections in each Hall dedicated to your growth and significance.

You can also access, as a Member, the Hall of Significance to join us as a Geographer or Licensee.

As a solopreneur you get to benefit from our networking, the community as a whole and, as a Member, selling your books, products etc. in our shop.

The Opportunities For Businesses

In 2022 we are expanding our corporate services with dedicated Account Managers for Corporate members of the Festival of Emotions.

For more on this see Chapter 8.

The Opportunities For Schools and Colleges

We have dedicated sections in each of the Halls where we feature experiences and services which are particularly suited to schools, universities, educational organisations and students.

Book Your Place

Come and visit the Festival of Emotions where you will find all that you need for your growth and significance, either as an individual a business or a corporation.

Contact Us

For more information on anything to do with Emotional Geography, The Festival of Emotions, Individual or Corporate enquiries or becoming a Geographer of Emotions please contact Ali or Marco:

ali@emotional-geography.com

marco@bertagniconsulting.com

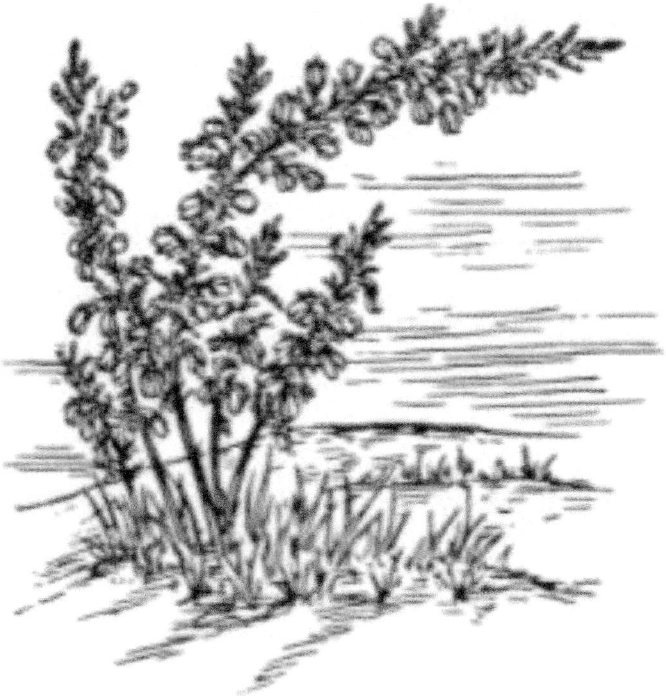

SPONSORS AND SUPPORTERS

This book, EMME, the Festival and our Community would not be possible without the support and investment of the following people and organisations.

Working together, mutual support and respect, celebrating each other's successes every single day. that is effective collaboration, that is EMME.

The original home of Emotional Geography as EMME and continuing to be our greatest benefactor and support. This is Marco Bertagni's international trade and lobbying consultancy. Supporting its clients in their business growth across the world *www.bertagniconsulting.com*

Ali Bagley Coaching provides the business development, web design and event organisation for the Festival. As a Business Coach and Best-Selling Author Ali helps your business to grow and thrive both through her courses and her one-to-one coaching services.
www.alibagleycoaching.co.uk

Marco Barozzi, Geographer of Emotions and Entrepreneur has leant his considerable expertise in event management to the building of this Festival. *https://www.expoconsulting.eu/en/*

Laurent Peters, an international strategy, organisation and change management expert has supported the Festival since its inception with his expertise and knowledge.

https://www.iponopi.com/en/home_en/

THE FLOW OF THE RIVER OF LIFE
Where will your River take you next?

Printed in Great Britain
by Amazon